CW00544975

# It's
# All Greek

Borrowed Words and their Histories

ALEXANDER TULLOCH

Bodleian Library
UNIVERSITY OF OXFORD

First published in 2019 by the Bodleian Library
Broad Street, Oxford OX1 3BG
www.bodleianshop.co.uk

ISBN 978 1 85124 505 5

Illustrations are from Alexandre de Laborde, *Collection
des vases grecs de M. le Comte de Lamberg*, 2 vols, 1813, 24.
Oxford, Bodleian Library, Douce Prints a.38-9

Cover design by Dot Little at the Bodleian Library
Designed and typeset in 10.5 on 14 Caslon by illuminati, Grosmont
Printed and bound in China by C&C Offset Printing Co. Ltd
on 120gsm Baijin pure woodfree FSC® paper

British Library Catalogue in Publishing Data
A CIP record of this publication is available from the British Library

# INTRODUCTION

Greek enjoys an enviable claim to fame. It is the longest continuously spoken and written language in Europe and can trace its origins back to beyond the late eighth century BCE when Homer was narrating the *Odyssey* and the *Iliad*. It is now also universally accepted among etymologists that a variety of Greek was in evidence as far back as 1500 BCE. If we set this alongside Latin, which dates from no earlier than the third century BCE, and the Celtic, Germanic and Slavonic languages, which date back no earlier than the sixth century CE, it is not difficult to appreciate that the singular longevity of Greek is nothing short of astonishing. Nor is it difficult to understand how a language of such antiquity should have influenced surrounding cultures and left its indelible mark on more recent languages, including English. It is no exaggeration to say that even today a speaker of English will use words (frequently unwittingly) which are either pure Greek or closely related to

Greek, and this applies not only to the inhabitants of the British Isles.

The spread of English throughout the world has been so successful that in countries such as the USA, Canada and Australia, where English is the predominant language, words of Greek origin will be spoken and written every single day. And if we add to these the indigenous populations of places such as China, Japan, India and Africa, who devote countless hours to the study and mastery of English, it is not difficult to appreciate that Ancient Greek is still being absorbed on a daily basis as students on every continent pore diligently over their textbooks.

The simple truth is that, as we go about our daily business, we are surrounded by Greek. If all the Greek words in English were to suddenly vanish we would have considerable difficulty in making ourselves understood. Consider, for example, a hospital. When we walk through the door and look at the signboard to find out where we need to go, we are immediately confronted by Greek words written in the Latin alphabet. The departments of paediatrics, orthopaedics, psychiatry, oncology, haematology, gynaecology and a host of others all take their names from Ancient Greek. And when doctors and nurses speak of a 'cardiac arrest', 'peptic ulcer', 'phlebitis', 'thrombosis', 'osteoarthritis', and so on, they are using word roots which would have been understood in the *agora,* or marketplace, of ancient Athens, Sparta or Corinth.

Once we have left the hospital we might decide to go to the cinema (a Greek word), the theatre (a Greek word) or pick up some groceries from the local supermarket, perhaps including marmalade, currants, butter (or, depending on our preference, margarine), words which are all, once again, Greek in origin. Then we might call in at the chemist, take a short cut home through the church grounds or pass by the local cemetery, without realizing that 'chemist', 'church' and 'cemetery' are modified Greek words. And as soon as we arrive home we will probably switch on the lamp and the television before answering the telephone, blissfully unaware that if it were not for Ancient Greek we would have to find other words for our domestic illumination, entertainment and means of communication. The plain fact is that, whether we realize it or not, we are deeply indebted to the language spoken in Athens 2,500 years ago for the ease and fluency with which we conduct our daily business in the modern world.

This is certainly not the first book to deal with the subject of Greek influence on English vocabulary, as the subject has fascinated linguists for decades. However, it is fair to say that other publications have dealt almost exclusively with the literary, scientific or scholarly contribution that Greek has made to English; the worlds of technology, science, medicine and so on are awash with Greek words which have come either directly or via Latin into English and have deservedly attracted the attention of etymologists.

My aim, however, has been to concentrate mainly on the 'surprises', by which I mean commonly used words which may raise even classicists' eyebrows with their Greek provenance or connections. Most educated people can recognize words such as 'mathematics', 'microphone', 'biology' and 'geometry' as being Greek, but how many are aware that 'purse', 'place', 'chimney', 'pirate' and even 'chair' are distantly related to words which Plato, Aristotle and Euripides would have understood? Not very many, I suspect.

It is difficult to say exactly how many Greek words there are in modern English, but recent estimates suggest something well in excess of 10,000. So, the question is, how did this situation arise? Part of the explanation, of course, is that the Ancient Greeks were an outward-looking, adventurous race who were not content to sit at home tending their goats and growing their crops from dawn until dusk every day. On the contrary, they got into their little boats and set out across the Aegean and Mediterranean seas; they colonized Sicily and southern Italy, had settlements in modern Egypt, southern Russia, Spain and Portugal, and mounted expeditions into Persia (modern Iran). Later, under the leadership of Alexander the Great (356–323 BCE), they conquered huge tracts of the known world, penetrating as far as India and Afghanistan. And in the countries where the Greeks put down their roots, their language and learning became firmly established and made a huge contribution to local, then

European and eventually world culture. Their dramatists, architects, philosophers and sculptors have bequeathed an incredible legacy from which people the world over still derive enormous benefit, intellectual stimulation and endless enjoyment.

Another factor involves the role of Greek learning in the early Church. The New Testament was originally written in Greek and the spread of Christianity facilitated the ever-increasing influence of the language throughout the world as more and more countries accepted its teachings. The result is that virtually every language throughout Europe is richly peppered with Greek words. And English, of course, has benefited just as much, and possibly even more, than other languages from the rich contribution Greek has made. Common words gifted to us by the expansion of Greek culture via religion include 'Bible', 'bishop', 'cathedral', 'chorus', 'priest' and 'choir', to name but a few.

And there is yet another historical process we have to take into consideration. The age of scientific discovery, which began around the mid-sixteenth century, witnessed an explosion of creativity and invention and an increasing reluctance to accept the teachings of the established Church without question. Great minds demanded to be set free to explore the world and the universe from a scientific perspective; as discoveries were made and inventions invented, new words had to be found to define and describe the new concepts, theories and contraptions that were now being spoken of and written about. In many cases, the thinkers and inventors of the day turned to Greek to fill the void, so that words such as 'machine', 'orthodox', 'dilemma', 'diagnosis', 'anthropology' and many more entered the English language from the sixteenth century onwards. And the practice of adopting Greek words into English as and when the need arises continues even today, so that a reliance on the supposition that 'the Greeks had a word for it' is as sound as ever it was.

# BORROWED WORDS
## AND THEIR HISTORIES

## MACRONS AND TRANSLITERATION

Macrons (diacritics on certain vowels) have been used in this book to indicate when the sound represented by a certain letter should be lengthened, so basically *o* is short (as in 'cop'), but *ō* is long as in 'cope'. In Greek words these diacritics indicate vowel lengthening as represented by different letters in the Greek alphabet. The letter *e* therefore is the equivalent of the Greek *epsilon* (ε), but *ē* represents *eta* (η); *o* represents *omicron* (o) and *ō* the letter *omega* (ω).

The Greek letter *upsilon* (υ) has proven a little problematic. Strictly speaking, *upsilon* corresponds to the English *u*, so the word for door, θυρα, should be transliterated as *thura*. However, the letter has traditionally been transliterated with a *y*, so that *psuchē* (ψυχη) now has a more recognizable form in English as 'psyche'. Generally, I have not followed tradition, but where the reader is likely to recognize the more conventional spelling I have provided both forms to avoid confusion.

The Greek letter *chi* (χ) has been transliterated throughout as *ch*, pronounced as the 'ch' in 'loch'. It is also worth noting that in Ancient Greek the combination *gks* (γξ) is pronounced 'nks' and the combination *gk* is pronounced as if it were written *nk*. In Greek the semi-colon serves as a question mark.

## Abysmal

If we describe something as being 'the pits' we are not all that far removed from the derivation of a more literary adjective, 'abysmal'. The derivative Greek term is *abussos* (ἄβυσσος), 'bottomless', a combination of *a-* (α-), 'without', and *bussos* (βυσσός), 'bottom', 'bottom of the sea'. So, linguistically speaking, an 'abysmal' performance is so bad that it is beyond understanding or 'unfathomable'.

The adjective appeared in English in the nineteenth century, derived from a much earlier noun, 'abysm', a thirteenth-century borrowing from the Old French *abisme*. This was derived from the Medieval Latin *abysmus*, a direct borrowing from the Greek.

The modern derivative 'abyss' did not appear in English until the sixteenth century.

# Academy

An 'academy' is now usually a school offering advanced or specialized education, although the word can also designate a learned society or institution.

The original academy or *akadēmeia* (ἀκαδήμεια) was an estate just outside Athens where Plato taught his students (the first 'academics') and founded a school of philosophy in the fifth century BCE, which survived until 529 CE when it was closed down by Emperor Justinian I. The inscription above the entrance reads: *ageōmetrētos mēdeis eisitō* (ἀγεωμέτρητος μηδεὶς εἰσίτω), 'Let nobody who knows no geometry enter here'. Tradition has it that the estate itself was named in honour of *Akadēmos* (Ἀκάδημος), a Greek hero thought to be buried nearby.

The word was first used in English in the sixteenth century.

# Acme

This word, so beloved of commercial organizations that wish to be thought of as 'the best', was adopted into English in the seventeenth century as a synonym for 'the highest point' or, more figuratively, 'the culmination'. It is a direct borrowing of the Greek *akmē* (ἀκμή), which had quite a variety of meanings. It could simply be a 'peak', a 'point' or the 'tip' of anything. But it could also signify height (literally and figuratively), so that expressions abound in Greek such as *akmē hēbēs* (ἀκμὴ ἤβης), 'the bloom of youth'; *akmē esti* (ἀκμή ἐστι), 'it is high time to'; and *ep'akmēs einai* (ἐπ' ἀκμῆς εἶναι), 'to be on the point of'.

It is also the origin of the dreaded affliction of youth: acne. And it appears that the association is due to nothing more than a scribal error. At some point in medieval times, or possibly earlier, a Latin scholar who was transferring the Greek expression into Latin misread one letter and thus produced a spelling error which has since been accepted as a word in its own right.

## *Acrobat*

We now use this word to define anyone who is skilled at performing gymnastic manoeuvres, but the original meaning was closer to what we would refer to as a 'tightrope walker'. It was first used in English in the nineteenth century, borrowed from the French term *acrobate* but traceable back to the Greek *akrobatēs* (ἀκροβατής), meaning 'one who walks on tiptoes'. The noun is a contraction of *akros* (ἄκρος), 'tip', 'point', and the verb *bainein* (βαίνειν), 'to go', 'to walk'.

The confusion between performing impressively physical movements on the ground and awe-inspiring feats on a tightrope probably arises from the derivative verb *akrobatein* (ἀκροβατεῖν), which could mean either 'to walk on tiptoe' or 'to climb up high above the ground'.

## Agony

'Agony' is derived from the Greek verb *agein* (ἄγειν), 'to lead', and its associated noun *agōn* (ἀγών), an assembly of people 'led' or gathered together to watch a contest of one sort or another. As contests in Ancient Greece usually involved intense, not to say brutal, struggle and competition a further noun developed, *agōnia* (ἀγωνία), meaning either 'a struggle for victory' or 'a wrestling match'. The association with extreme physical pain entered English in the seventeenth century.

## Alms

Not a very common word nowadays but not too long ago it was generally used to denote charitable donations and gifts handed out by the better off to the poor. As late as the 1960s the hospital official responsible for patients' non-medical welfare was known as the 'almoner'.

In Old English the word *ælmesse* meant 'almsgiving' and was a derivative noun, via Church Latin, from the Greek *eleēmosunē* (ἐλεημοσύνη), 'pity', 'mercy'. This was a derivative of the basic noun *eleos* (ἔλεος), 'pity', 'compassion', from the verb *eleein (*ἐλεεῖν), 'to feel pity towards'.

## Alphabet

Basically, an alphabet is a system of recording spoken language and allowing it to be committed to a writing surface. English, along with many other languages in the world, uses what is usually referred to as the Latin alphabet, even though this is essentially a modified form of the Greek.

The Phoenician linear alphabet, usually accepted as the precursor of modern western alphabets, began life in the Middle East around the eleventh century BCE when the Phoenicians devised a form of script that allowed people to keep records in such a way that the spoken language maintained a close affinity with the written. This was adopted by the early Greeks *c*.750 BCE; the form of the letters they devised not only remained more or less the same over the centuries but has also influenced the writing systems in many parts of the world. The Archaic Greek alphabet formed the basis of the Modern Greek, the Latin (or Roman) and the Slavonic alphabets.

The word 'alphabet' itself is derived from a combination of the names of the first two Greek letters, *alpha* (ἄλφα) and *bēta* (βῆτα), which stand for all twenty-four letters that make up the Greek 'alphabet'.

## Ambrosia

In the 1550s the word 'ambrosia' entered the English language as a descriptive noun for just about anything that tasted delicious. Its immediate antecedent was the Latin *ambrosia*, but this had been borrowed from the Greek *ambrosia* (ἀμβροσία), usually translated as 'the

food of the gods' but meaning more correctly 'the food of the immortals'. By the time John Milton published his epic *Paradise Lost* in 1667 the word had become so well established in English that he was able to refer, with considerable poetic effect, to Paradise and its 'water from the ambrosial fount'.

The derivative Greek noun was *brotos* (βροτός), 'man', 'mortal', and its opposite *ambrotos* (ἄμβροτος) was 'an immortal'. Strictly speaking, *ambrosia* (ἀμβροσία) is the feminine form of the adjective of *ambrosios* (ἀμβρόσιος), 'pertaining to the immortals', 'divine', and is part of the phrase *ambrosia edōdē* (ἀμβροσία ἐδωδή), 'divine food'. And in both Latin and Greek mythology 'ambrosia' is also regarded as the elixir of life.

## WHAT THE GODS DRANK

If ambrosia was the food of the gods, their drink was known to the Ancient Greeks as *nektar*, or nectar.

The word has some fascinating associations in modern English. A particularly tasty drink can be described as being 'pure nectar', and among the scientific community 'nectar' refers to the sugary liquid secreted by plants and from which bees make honey. But the Old English term for this substance was *mildeaw*, or, to give it its modern spelling, 'mildew', the first syllable of which is taken straight from the Greek *meli-*, 'honey'. This explains why 'honeydew' is an alternative term for 'mildew'.

The word 'honey' in English can be traced back through the Germanic languages to an earlier form *hunig*, cognate with the Greek *knēkos* (κνηκός), an adjective meaning 'pale yellow'.

## Amethyst

Most people probably think of an 'amethyst' as simply a semi-precious purple-coloured stone guaranteed to add adornment to even the drabbest of clothes. But to the Ancient Greeks the stone was worn (some sources say sucked) as a supposed antidote to the effects of overindulging in the fruit of the vine. It made its way into English in the late thirteenth century when it appeared as *ametist*, from the Old French *ametist*, both being derived from the Latin *amethystus*. But the Romans had acquired it from the Greek *amethustos* (ἀμέθυστος), meaning 'not intoxicated'. The word was a combination of *a-* (ἀ), 'not', and *methuskein* (μεθύσκειν), 'to make someone drunk', from *methu* (μέθυ), 'wine', a noun directly related to the English word 'mead'.

In the Middle Ages the French scribes of the day reinstated the 'th' of the Latin spelling, which was mirrored in English in the sixteenth century when 'amethyst' replaced *ametist*.

## Anathema

There can be few better examples in etymology of how a word can completely change its original meaning than this one. Since the early seventeenth century it has been used in English to denote something dreadful, abhorrent or, as it is often described, 'an accursed thing'. In the original Greek, however, it meant something that had been offered up to the gods and would therefore have had nothing but positive associations. For the early Christians, though, it was tainted with false religious beliefs and had nothing but negative implications, which account for the meaning we attach to the word today.

The Greek word was *anathema* (ἀνάθεμα), 'an offering to the gods', based on *ana-* (ἀνα-), 'up', 'upwards', and *tithenai* (τίθέναι), 'to put', 'to place'. The literal meaning of 'anathema', therefore, is 'something placed on high'.

## Anecdote

In the sixth century CE the Palestinian scholar and diarist Procopius wrote an account of the scurrilous goings-on at the Byzantine court of Emperor Justinian (483–565 CE). According to Procopius, Justinian and his wife Theodora indulged in some pretty unseemly, even shocking, behaviour, and the scholar's account was considered unsuitable reading material for the general public. Hence his writings were not published and were referred to in Greek as *anecdota* (ἀνέκδοτα), literally 'the things not given out'. The word *anecdota* comprises three parts: *an-* (αν-), 'not', + *ek* (ἐκ), 'out', + *dota* (δοτα), 'things given', from the verb *didonai* (διδόναι), 'to give'.

In the 1670s English borrowed the French *anecdote*, which conveyed much the same idea as the title of Procopius' writings. They denoted private accounts and stories written for small groups of selected people who enjoyed literature of a more salacious nature than was available to the populace as a whole. By the mid-eighteenth century, however, the word had lost most of its sensational flavour and had acquired the meaning we attach to it today: a pithy, amusing story.

## Angle

English has used the word 'angle' to define the space between two intersecting or touching lines since the fourteenth century. It is derived from the Latin word *angulus*, 'corner', and related to the earlier Greek adjective *ankulos* (ἀγκύλος), meaning 'crooked' or 'curved'. This was also the adjective used to describe the 'hooked' shape of an eagle's beak.

But there are further twists in the history and evolution of this word. The basic Greek form showed up in Old English as *angel*, meaning a 'fish hook', no doubt because of the hook's crooked shape. And there is a further echo of Greek again here: the Greek for 'to go fishing with hook and line' was *agkurizein* (ἀγκυρίζειν), which offers a parallel with modern English references to the practice of catching fish (or attempting to) as either 'fishing' or 'angling'.

Other words in English closely related to the original Greek are 'ankle' (a 'bend' in the leg) and 'anchor' (a 'hooked' implement designed to secure a boat to the river- or seabed).

## Anorexia

The Greeks had a verb *oregein* (ὀρέγειν), which meant, quite simply, 'to reach out for', 'to stretch out and grasp'. With the passage of time the verb acquired the more figurative meaning of yearning or longing for something. The same verb produced the noun *orexis* (ὄρεξις), 'longing', 'desire', and the later addition of the negative prefix *an-* (ἀν-) produced the Late Latin *anorexia* and changed the meaning to 'absence of longing' and, more specifically, 'loss of appetite'. So, if we describe someone as being 'anorexic' what we are literally saying is that he or she is unwilling 'to reach out' for something to eat.

The word has been used in English since 1598.


# Anthology

Few people would understand this word as being anything other than a book containing a collection of poems or short prose extracts, but it has only had this meaning in English since the 1630s. The original Greek word *anthologia* (ἀνθολογία) was made up of *anthos* (ἄνθος), 'flower', and *legein* (λέγειν), 'to collect', and so meant 'a gathering of flowers' or 'a nosegay'. The usual explanation for such an apparently drastic shift of meaning is that the early publishers thought collections of delightful poetry were as charming as little bunches of flowers.


# Anthropology

The word entered English in the 1590s, from the Late Latin *anthropologia*, a noun based on the Greek adjective *anthrōpologos* (ἀνθρωπολόγος), 'speaking of man'. It was seized upon by learned men of the day who needed a word to describe the emerging science based on an objective study of humankind in all its various manifestations. This was the time, we should remember, when Alexander

Pope (1688–1744) was telling us that 'the proper study of Mankind is Man'.

The Late Latin form *anthropologia* was adopted from the Greek *anthrōpos* (ἄνθρωπος), 'man', and *logos* (λόγος), 'word', 'argument' or 'the study of'.

> *ti dē hoi anthrōpoi; theoi thnētoi.*
> *Ti de dē hoi theoi; anthrōpoi athanatoi*
>
> τί δὴ οἱ ἄνηρωποι; θεοὶ θνητοί.
> Τί δὲ δὴ οἱ θεοί; ἄνθρωποι ἀθάνατοι
>
> 'what then are men? Mortal gods.
> So, what then are gods? Immortal men.'
>
> HERACLITUS OF EPHESUS

## *Apothecary*

J.K. Rowling, with her Harry Potter novels featuring wizards' shops known as 'apothecaries', can perhaps be credited with reviving a term which fell out of fashion some time in the early nineteenth century. Shakespeare included an apothecary in *Romeo and Juliet* (*c.*1591) and *King Lear* (*c.*1605), and it was still widely applied to purveyors of spices and herbal remedies in 1617 when grocers and apothecaries emerged as distinct professions. From about 1800 the term 'apothecary' gave way to 'chemist', although its use as a professional designation continued for some time; the poet John Keats, for instance, qualified as an apothecary in 1816.

The original 'apothecaries', however, were simply traders who 'put goods to one side' – mainly spices. The word entered English in the fourteenth century, borrowed from the Old French *apotecaire*, derived from the Late Latin *apothecarius*, 'a store keeper'. The source of both words was the Greek verb *apotithenai* (ἀποτιθέναι), 'to put away', 'to put to one side', and the related noun *apothēkē* (ἀποθήκη), which could mean 'a barn', 'a granary' or generally anywhere where goods were stored. By the seventeenth century the meaning had narrowed and had become a term for specialist traders who dealt mainly in drugs.

## Architecture

Britain boasts many examples of magnificent architecture which date back over a thousand years, but the word 'architecture' and 'architect' have only existed in English since the 1560s. In Anglo-Saxon times the equivalent of an architect would have been a *heahcraeftiga*, or 'high crafter', but after the Norman Conquest this was gradually replaced by *architectour*, 'a superintendent', from the Latin *architectus*, 'master builder', 'chief workman'. It was not until the sixteenth century that the modern concept of an architect being more concerned with planning and design emerged.

The Latin *architectus* was a development of the Greek *architektōn* (ἀρχιτέκτων), who, in ancient Athens, was a master builder or director of works (probably the equivalent of a foreman). And this word was a combination of *archōn* (ἄρχων), 'chief' or 'ruler', and *tektōn* (τέκτων), a rather loose term which was applied to almost any craftsman, but defined particularly a worker in wood, a carpenter or a builder.

Another related adjective is 'tectonic', as in the Earth's 'tectonic plates'. These are layers of rock that form the basis of the 'architectural' structure or the Earth's surface.

## *Archive*

Historians love archives. Their work can involve hours sifting through documents and files for unknown or long-forgotten facts to include in a new academic paper or book. The rest of us, however, are probably more familiar these days with the 'archive' feature on our computers where we can store files and emails we have little use for immediately but wish to retain, just in case they are needed in the future.

The word entered English in or around 1600 as a borrowing from French, which had been using the word *archif* as a depository for important official documents since the previous century. The French had borrowed the word from Late Latin *archivum* (with its plural form *archiva*), acquired from the Greek *archeia* (ἀρχεῖα). In ancient Athens these were the public records, so called because they were official documents stored for safe-keeping in the *archeion* (ἀρχεῖον), a building which we would probably refer to as the town hall. It was the residence of the *archōn* (ἄρχων), an official ranking roughly with a modern mayor or magistrate.

## *Argos*

A certain high-street chain-store company in the UK adopted this name some time ago as its trademark. From the editorial of a staff magazine of the time we get a good idea of why the name was chosen. The Greek word *argos* (ἀργός) meant 'speedy' or 'bright', particularly when associated with flashes of sunlight reflected off a limpid pool or running water. Furthermore, a name recalling the oldest continuously inhabited town in Europe, Argos, could offer nothing but an advantageous association for a firm whose management was intent on a long and prosperous trading future.

But there is a sting in the tail here as there is another Greek word, also *argos* (ἀργός), meaning 'lazy' or 'bone idle'. The confusion arises because this second 'argos' is an adjective derived from the contraction of *a-* (ἀ), 'without', 'lacking', and the noun *ergon* (ἔργον), 'work'. When put together, the resultant adjective is certainly not suggestive of a speedy work ethic or rapid efficiency in dealing with customers.

The gas known as 'argon' is directly related to the second 'argos'. It is one of the 'noble' gases (so-called because they show no tendency to mix with other gases) and is 'inert' – that is, without any inherent action.

## Aristocracy

To the Ancient Greeks the word *aristokratia* (ἀριστοκρατία) essentially meant 'power in the hands of the best', and by 'best' they usually meant 'best born' or 'the sons of the nobility'. The word comprised two elements: *aristos* (ἄριστος), 'best', and *kratos* (κράτος), 'power', 'authority'.

But this is by no means the end of the story; a quick glance at etymologically related words reveals much about the manner in which the Greek mind worked. Grammatically, the word *aristos* (ἄριστος) was the superlative form of the adjective *agathos* (ἀγαθός), 'good', but this was a later development of the language. The original meaning of *aristos* was 'bravest'; it was a close relative of the plural noun *aristeia* (ἀριστεία), 'heroic deeds', 'deeds of great valour'. Both of these expressions were connected with the words *arrēn* (ἄρρην), 'male', 'strong', 'masculine', and *Arēs* (Ἄρης), 'Arēs', the god of war and destruction. Another related noun was *aretē* (ἀρετή), which, by the fifth and fourth centuries BCE, signified excellence in any field or activity. For Homer (eighth century BCE) it referred simply to manhood and bravery on the field of battle.

Putting all this information together, the inescapable conclusion is that the concept of 'the best' for the Ancient Greeks was originally epitomized by masculine values and martial prowess. And there is a parallel here with the Roman world: our word 'virtue', meaning merit or high moral conviction, is closely related to the word 'virile', and both derive from *vir*, the Latin for 'man'.

## Arithmetic

English has been using this word to define the act of counting and calculating since the thirteenth century. It was borrowed from the Latin *arithmetica*, which itself was a borrowing from the Greek expression *arithmetikē techne* (ἀριθμετική τέχνη), 'the art of numbering'.

The derivative verb in play here is *arithmein* (ἀριθμεῖν), 'to count', and the noun *arithmos* (ἀριθμός), 'number'.

The closely associated verb 'to calculate' also has a Greek derivation. It is based on the noun *chalix* (χάλιξ), meaning 'a pebble', and is a reference to the most basic method of counting – that is, by using small stones or pebbles. It made its way into English via the Latin *calx*, stone, and the distinctly recognizable *calculus*.

## Arthritis

Most people probably think of this word as a noun, but strictly speaking it comes from an adjective, *arthritikos* (ἀρθρῑτικός), meaning 'relating to the joints'. *Arthritis nosos* (ἀρθρῖτις νόσος) means 'joint disease', 'disease relating to the joints', from *nosos* (νόσος), 'sickness', 'disease', and *arthron* (ἄρθρον), 'joint' or 'joint socket'. From this we get our word for the painful medical condition.

> *iatros adoleschos epi nosō nosos*
>
> ἰατρὸς ἀδόλεσχος ἐπὶ νόσῳ νόσος
>
> 'a talkative doctor is a disease on top of a disease'
>
> MENANDER

## Asphalt

At the mention of the word 'asphalt' most of us will think of the tarry black substance used to give roads a smooth and safe surface on which to drive. And herein lies a clue to the origin of the word.

We have used the word to define road covering since 1847, although it was known in English as early as the fourteenth century (when it was spelled *asphaltoun*) from references in the Bible. In ancient times *asphaltos* (ἄσφαλτος), as it was known in Greek, was a bituminous substance that appeared on the surface of the waters near Babylon and was used by local builders as a kind of mortar. Walls built with bricks secured by 'asphalt' were known to be secure and unlikely to collapse.

The associated adjective in Greek was *asphalēs* (ἀσφαλής), which generally had the meaning of 'secure', 'assured', and a person so described was thought of as being reliable, trustworthy and a staunch friend. The derivative verb was *sphallein* (σφαλλεῖν), generally meaning 'to topple' but more specifically, in wrestling, 'to trip' or 'to fell' an opponent, so anything considered *asphaltos* (ἄσφαλτος) was literally unlikely to collapse.

The idea of security survives in the modern use of the word; visitors to Greece even today will see shop fronts and commercial buildings offering *aspháleia zōēs* (ασφάλεια ζωής), 'life insurance'.

## *Asphyxia*

As a medical term for what most people would think of as suffocation, 'asphyxia' has been used in English since *c*.1705. But there is more than just a slight problem connected with its history and etymology. When eighteenth-century doctors used the term, they were indicating that they could no longer detect a pulse in their patient. It was not until 1778 that it acquired the meaning we attach to the word today – that is, suffocation caused by insufficient oxygen reaching the bloodstream. The associated verb 'asphyxiate' and noun 'asphyxiation' are first recorded in English in 1818 and 1849 respectively.

The derivation of the word is the Greek *asphuksia* (ἀσφυξία), 'a lack of a pulse', derived from *a-* (ἀ), 'without', and *sphugmos* (σφυγμός), 'throbbing', from the verb *sphuzein* (σφύζειν), 'to throb', 'to beat' (referring to the pulse). The related Greek plural noun *sphuzonta* (σφύζοντα), literally 'things that throb', meant veins or arteries.

What is most surprising about the adoption of the word into English in the eighteenth century is that is appears to reflect a lack of anatomical knowledge among the members of the medical profession. Victims of suffocation do not cease to have a pulse for some time after breathing has stopped.

## Astronaut

The man credited with the first use of the word 'astronaut' is the English science-fiction writer Percy Greg, who in 1880 published his novel *Across the Zodiac*. This is an imaginary account of a journey to Mars and the narrator's encounters with strange little men who refuse to believe that he has come from a world other than their own. Greg named the spacecraft which had made the fantastic journey through time and space the *Astronaut*, but by 1929 the word was being applied not to the vehicle but to the intrepid 'space travellers' whose interstellar odysseys were starting to look like an ever-increasing possibility.

The word itself it based on the Greek for star, *astēr* (ἀστήρ), and *nautēs* (ναύτης), sailor, so that an 'astronaut' is strictly speaking somebody who 'sails among the stars'.

Interestingly, when extraterrestrial flight became a reality in the 1960s the Americans opted for the term 'astronaut' to describe the men and women who reached for the stars, but the Russians preferred to call their explorers 'cosmonauts' – that is, 'those who sail through the cosmos'.

Other terms for the various objects hurtling around above our heads in space which have names derived from Greek:

*Planet* from the Greek noun *planē*, 'wandering', and the verb *planasthai*, 'to wander'. The Greeks referred to the planets as *planētes asteres*, 'wandering stars'.

*Comet* This was first recorded in English *c.* 1200 as a borrowing from the Latin *cometa*, which in turn was derived from the Greek *astēr komētēs*, 'long-haired star'. The derivative noun *komē* simply meant 'hair'; the description is a reference to the long trail that is the distinguishing mark of a comet.

*Moon* is cognate with the Greek *mēnē*, 'moon', and its associated noun *mēn*, 'month'. Both can trace their origins back to an Indo-European root meaning 'to measure', the inference being that the 'moon' was originally thought of as a 'measurer' of time.

# Asylum

The word as we use it today is the Latin version of the Greek *asulon* (ἄσυλον), 'the right not to be harmed' and 'free from plunder'. The associated verb *sulan* (συλᾶν) was a military term meaning specifically 'to strip the weapons off an enemy' once he had been slain on the field of battle. In its plural form, *sulai* (σῦλαι), it defined the right either to seize the ship or cargo from foreign merchants or to carry out reprisals against an enemy in time of war.

The idea of an 'asylum' as a safe place in which to seek refuge dates from the 1640s, and as a protective shelter, such as a 'lunatic asylum', from the eighteenth century.

## Athlete

There are two closely related Greek nouns associated with the derivation of this word. An *athlon* (ἄθλον) was a prize awarded to the winner of a sporting contest, and an *athlos* (ἄθλος) was a struggle or contest between rival contestants, whether on the sports field or on the field of battle. The associated verbs were *athleuein* (ἀθλεύειν), 'to struggle', 'to contend for a prize', and *athlein* (ἀθλεῖν), meaning 'to contend' or simply 'to be an athlete'.

From a historical and cultural point of view it is interesting to note how the ideas of sport and combat were inseparable in the minds of the Ancient Greeks.

## THE LABOURS OF HERCULES

What we normally refer to as the 'Labours of Hercules' were known in Greek as *Herakleous athloi* ('Ηρακλέους ἄθλοι) and are an account in Greek mythology of the twelve tasks the hero Heraklēs (Hercules was the Romans' name for him) was required to complete as a punishment for having been tricked into killing all twelve of his children. The labours, or *athloi*, were:

1. Slay the Nemean lion.
2. Slay the nine-headed Lernaean hydra.
3. Capture the Cerynaiean hind.
4. Capture the Erymanthean boar.
5. Clean out the Augean stables in a single day.
6. Kill the Stymphalian birds.
7. Capture the Cretan bull.
8. Steal the mares of Diomedes.
9. Bring back the girdle of Hippolyta, Queen of the Amazons.
10. Fetch the cattle belonging to the monster Geryon.
11. Steal the apples of the Hesperides.
12. Capture and return with Cerberus.

All twelve tasks had to be completed within twelve years, and of course our hero managed it.

## Atom

From an etymological point of view, an atom is simply something that cannot be cut. The Greek word, from which the English is derived, is *atomos* (ἄτομος), an adjective meaning 'uncut', from the prefix *a-* (ἀ-), 'un-', and the verb *temnein* (τέμνειν), 'to cut'. The basic idea

### ATOMIC THEORY

In the fifth century BCE in Athens two philosophers, Leucippos and his pupil Democritos, were the leading lights among the thinkers known as the Atomists. These were people who believed that all matter was composed of nothing but atoms and void. They took their thinking a step further and decided that nothing composed of atoms really existed and that nothing exists apart from atoms bouncing off each other. This led them to take yet another step further to the conclusion that, as any given body is made up of an infinite number of atoms in constant motion, there must be an infinite number of worlds and even universes also in a state of perpetual motion. Astonishingly, this is not all that far from what many cosmologists believe today.

Another use of the term 'atom' in classical and medieval times was as an infinitesimally small unit of time. An example of this is seen in the Bible when Paul, in his first letter to the Corinthians (15:52), says *en atomō, en rhipē ophthalmou* (ἐν ἄτομος ἐν ῥιπῇ ὀφθαλμου), 'in a moment, in the twinkling of an eye'.

is that if we take an object and cut it in half, and the two halves in half again, and so on, eventually we will arrive at a fraction of the original whole that is so small it cannot possibly be divided again. This is the 'atom'.

The word was first used in English in the sixteenth century, when it was the term for the smallest body incapable of further division. In the seventeenth century it was used by men of science as a definition of the ultimate particle in matter, but by the nineteenth it was being used again to define the indivisibly finite. In the twentieth century, of course, scientists discovered how to cut the uncuttable and split the atom, and we have the adjective 'subatomic' to describe the resulting particles.

## Austerity

This word is a favourite of politicians who feel the need to warn us all of the harsh, even burdensome, times ahead. And if we add that the measures they put forward to make us all tighten our belts are likely to leave a bitter taste in our mouths, we are not very far removed from the original meaning of the word. By the 1580s the word was synonymous in English with 'severe self-denial' or 'ascetic lifestyle' and a few centuries later, during the Second World War, it was a fitting description for the government policy of producing nothing more than the essentials needed for the survival of the nation.

English first adopted the word in the fourteenth century from Latin (via French), which had the adjective *austerus*, meaning 'sour', 'harsh on the tongue' or, metaphorically, 'gloomy', 'difficult to bear'. In Old French the word *austerité*, in certain contexts, meant simply 'cruelty'.

But the Latin word had made its way through time and space from the Greek *austēros* (αὐστηρός). This was an adjective originally applied to the tart, sharp fruits and wines which left a bitter or rough taste on the tongue. It was itself derived from the verb *auein* (αὔειν), meaning 'to dry', 'to wither' or 'to singe', 'to set something on fire'.

## Bacteria

It is not always realized that this is actually the plural of *bacterium*, the Latin version of the Greek word *baktērion* (βακτήριον), a term coined by the German naturalist Christian Ehrenberg in the nineteenth century. He chose the word deliberately because the minute life forms he observed through a microscope resembled *baktēria* (βακτηρία), 'little sticks'. A closely related word, 'bacillus', derives from the Latin for a walking stick, *baculum*.

## Barbarian

Plato divided humanity into two groups: Hellenes (i.e. the Greeks) and Barbarians. Basically this meant, on the one hand, people who spoke Greek and, on the other, people whose language sounded like 'baa-baa-baa'. The resultant adjective was *barbaros* (βάρβαρος), meaning 'strange' or 'foreign'. By the time the word had made its way into English in the fifteenth century it had acquired the more pejorative meanings we associate with it today.

But there is an interesting etymological by-product. The edible plant we refer to as 'rhubarb' is a direct relative and comprises the Greek *Rha* (Ῥα), a river in modern Russia now called the Volga, and *barbaros* (βάρβαρος), 'foreign'. Hence the word originally defined the 'foreign' or 'strange' plant that grew along the banks of the Volga.

## Baritone

Until *c.*1600 a male singer with a deep sonorous voice was simply said to have a deep voice. At the very beginning of the seventeenth century the word 'baritone' was adopted into English from the Italian *baritono*, itself a borrowing from the Greek *barutonos* (βαρύτονος), meaning 'heavy' or 'deep sounding'. The adjective was a combination of *barus* (βαρύς), 'heavy', and *tonos* (τόνος), a noun applied to just about anything that had been pulled and tightened; the derivative verb was *teinein* (τείνειν), 'to stretch'. No doubt the Ancient Greeks realized that there was a relationship between a sound and the degree to which the source of the sound had been stretched. Proof of this can be seen in the fact that *barutonos*, in addition to 'deep sounding', also meant 'stretched tight'.

But there is a problem here. The Greek expression implies that the more a cord, for example, is stretched the deeper will be the sound it produces when plucked. But physics tells us that this is simply not the case, and as the tension increases so the pitch of any sound produced rises.

## Basil

The aromatic plant which occupies such an important position in the panoply of herbs and spices to be found in almost every kitchen throughout the land takes its name from the Greek *basilikos* (βασιλικός), 'royal', and derivative noun *basileus* (βασιλεύς), 'king'. There is some disagreement concerning the royal connection to the herb: some say it is because 'basil' is the 'king of herbs'; others maintain that it is so called because it was used in the ancient world for making a king's perfumes. Either way, 'basil' was known in Ancient Greece as the *basilikon phuton* (βασιλικόν φυτόν), 'royal plant'.

Another word directly descended from the Greek for 'king' is 'basilica'. Some churches in the western world are now designated as 'basilicas' but the originals were based on the Greek term *basileios stoa* (βασίλειος στοά), 'king's portico' or 'royal cloister'. Architecturally, such a building would have consisted of an oblong hall with columns or pillars at regular intervals down the aisles, a design that provided the model for many of the churches built after the advent of Christianity.

After his conversion to Christianity, the Emperor Constantine decided that the seven principal churches in Rome should be known as 'basilicas'.

The word has been used in English since the fifteenth century.

*Erōs tōn theōn basileue*

Ἔρως τῶν θεῶν βασίλευε

'Love is the king of the gods'

PLATO, *SYMPOSIUM*

## Bomb

Unfortunately, this is a word that features regularly in our everyday lives with far more regularity than most of us would wish.

It has featured in English since the seventeenth century, when it was borrowed from the Italian, which had the word *bomba*. This in turn had its origin in the Greek *bombos* (βόμβος), any 'deep, hollow sound' (linguists define it as being 'echoic' as the noun is really just an imitation of the noise itself). The same Greek noun also gave us the 'bumblebee'.

## Bombastic

A bombastic speaker is one who can usually be described as liking the sound of his or her own voice and is prone to peppering speeches with unnecessary verbiage, flowery conceits and irrelevant rhetorical language. In short, he pads out what he is trying to say so that it lasts far longer than it should. And 'pads out' is a clue to the origin of the word.

The word 'bombast' first entered English in the 1560s and became the usual term for the padding in clothes as well as the stuffing in furniture; its application to declamatory speeches dates from the 1580s. But its origin lies with the Ancient Greeks, whose word *bombuks* (βόμβυξ) meant, originally, 'a silk worm' but was later applied to the silk itself.

## Box

It is impossible to say exactly when this word entered English; all we can say with any degree of certainty is that the word was known in late Anglo-Saxon Britain. We can also say with confidence that there is a very close relationship between 'box' as a container and 'box' as an evergreen shrub. In fact, it appears that the original 'boxes' were so called because they had been made out of 'box' wood.

The word is directly linked to the Late Latin *buxis* and the Latin *buxus*, both of which were terms for the shrub and also borrowings of the Greek *puksos* (πύξος), with the same meaning.

The association with small containers also originated in Greece, where early carpenters used the wood from the box tree to fashion containers in which documents and valuables could be placed for safekeeping. And such a container was known as a *puksis* (πύξις), which was later anglicized as 'box'.

The Greeks had several expressions equating to the English 'taking coals to Newcastle'; one of them was *pukson eis Kutōron agein* (πύξον ἐις Κύτωρον ἄγειν), meaning literally 'to take a box tree/box wood to Kutoros', a town in Paphlagonia in Asia Minor. No doubt Kutoros was famed throughout the Greek-speaking world for the quality or quantity of the box wood produced there.

The use of the term in English as a separate compartment in a theatre dates from *c*.1600 and the expression 'box office' was first recorded in 1786.

## *Boy*

It will probably come as a bit of a shock to most people, but some etymologists argue that the English word 'boy' is distantly related to the Ancient Greek for an ox or cow.

As late as the thirteenth century the word was applied to a youth or man of low estate, and in particular to a young male servant; it was not until the fourteenth century that 'boy' became the general term for a young male child.

The Middle English spelling of the word was *boi(e)*, derived from the Old French *embuier*, 'to fetter', from the Latin *boia*, a fetter, particularly of the type worn around the neck. And the Latin word was derived from the Greek *bous* (βοῦς), 'ox', and *boeiē* (βοείη), meaning both 'ox hide' and 'a rope made of twisted ox hide'.

It would appear, therefore, that the 'boys' of the twenty-first century take their name from the Ancient Greek young males who were kept as slaves and prevented from running away from their masters' estates by being restrained with ox-hide fetters.

## Bulimia

The term is now used in medical circles to describe an eating disease characterized by a voracious appetite and binge eating followed by feelings of guilt and self-induced vomiting. To the Ancient Greeks, however, it was simply synonymous with the pangs of extreme hunger.

The Greek term *boulimia* (βουλιμία) comprised two nouns: *bous* (βοῦς), 'ox', and *limos* (λιμός), 'hunger', so that someone described as 'bulimic' was originally thought to be so hungry that they could eat as much as an ox.

## Bureau

In a domestic setting, a bureau nowadays tends to denote a chest of drawers with a flap that can be pulled down to serve as a writing surface, and this is the meaning the word has had since 1770. In the 1690s it became the usual term, borrowed from French, for a writing desk with drawers, but was so called really because of the material with which it was covered. In the seventeenth century French cabinetmakers took to covering their handiwork with dark red, flame-coloured coarse baize known as *burel*, derived from the Late Latin *burra,* a rough, shaggy woollen garment, and the adjective *burrus*, 'reddish brown'.

The ultimate source of the French and Late Latin terms, however, is the Greek *purros* (πυρρός), meaning 'dark red', 'tawny' or 'flame coloured'. And the adjective was derived from the noun *pur* (πῦρ), meaning 'fire'.

Soon after the first bureaux appeared in the working environment, the rooms in which they were assembled for the sake of efficiency and convenience were perhaps also referred to as bureaux; hence the noun refers to both the furniture itself and the office or room in which it is found. As a term for a division of government (particularly common in France and the USA), 'bureau' dates back to 1720.


## *Butter*

It is not known exactly when this word entered English but it must have been known in Anglo-Saxon times, as the Old English term for it was *butere.* The Romans referred to it as *butyrum.* There is some discussion about the origin of this word, but the most authoritative etymologists agree that it is from a Greek word, *bouturon* (βούτυρον), derived from *bous* (βοῦς), 'ox', and *turos* (τυρός), 'cheese'. The literal meaning of 'butter' therefore is 'cow cheese'.

## Carol

The religious songs Christians sing in church are referred to as hymns. But the hymns especially reserved for Christmas are known by another term, 'carols', and their origin has more to do with dancing than with singing.

The derivative Greek word was *choraulēs* (χοραύλης), a 'flute player', comprising *choros* (χορός), 'dance', and *aulos* (αὐλός), 'flute', and the original activity associated with the word was 'dancing to the accompaniment of music played on a flute'. The word's association with Christmas festivities dates only from the sixteenth century.

## Carrot

The humble carrot as we know it originated in the area of the world around what is modern Afghanistan. There had been a white carrot (frequently confused with the parsnip) commonly used in Europe in antiquity, but it fell out of favour and had to be reintroduced by the Arabs at about the time of the Crusades. This 'new' carrot was a mutation of the Arab purple variety.

The word entered English in the 1530s as a borrowing from the Middle French *carrotte*, from an earlier Latin *carota*, and this in turn was taken directly from the Greek *karōton* (χαρωτόν). Many etymologists are convinced that the Indo-European root in play here is *\*ker*, 'horn' or 'head'. If they are correct (and there is little reason to suspect that they are not), it means that the word 'carrot' is related to words such as 'corn' (i.e. callous), 'horn' and even the English county of Cornwall, which was named by the Romans, whose word *cornū* meant a 'horn' but also a 'promontory'.

As a name for a colour, the word was first used in English after the 1670s and for a while its use was restricted to describing the colour of a person's hair.

## Catalogue

In the modern world a catalogue is usually a book or booklet issued by a commercial organization detailing the products it is offering the public for sale. The original Greek meaning, however, was predominantly military, as a *katalogos* (χατάλογος) was a list of people eligible for military service. It comprises the basic verb *legein* (λέγειν), 'to gather', and *kata-* (χατα), an intensifying prefix, producing the compound verb *katalegein* (χαταλέγειν), 'to gather up'.

The word has been used in English since the fifteenth century to mean basically 'a list'.

## Catapult

There was a time, not so very long ago, when no self-respecting schoolboy would have been seen without a catapult protruding from his pocket. Now the word is largely restricted to metaphorical usage, such as when we speak of a teenager being 'catapulted' to stardom, fame and fortune.

The original Greek word was a combination of *kata* (κατά), normally meaning 'down' but also, as in this case, 'against', and the verb *pallein* (πάλλειν), 'to hurl'. A *katapeltēs* (καταπέλτης) was an instrument of war used for propelling huge arrows or bolts at an enemy from a device resembling a giant crossbow.

In the sixteenth century, a 'catapult' was an English military term for a contraption designed for hurling missiles at an enemy; its association with forked sticks and pieces of elastic designed to fire off small stones dates from the nineteenth century.

## Catastrophe

The Greek word καταστροφή (*katastrophē*), formed from two words, κατὰ (*kata*), 'down', and στροφή (*strophē*), 'a turn' or 'a twist', originally meant something far less scary than its modern equivalent in English. It was simply an agricultural term used by farmers turning over the soil and no doubt mixing it with good strong manure to ensure an abundant harvest the following year. Our use of the word as a synonym for 'calamity' retains something of the idea of the things being 'turned over' or even 'overturned'.

In Greek drama the καταστροφή (*katastrophē*) was the term used for what we now normally refer to as the 'dénouement' or unravelling of the plot.

## Category

The origin of this word lies in the Ancient Greek worlds of both commerce and law. In Greek cities such as Athens and Sparta, the *agora* (ἀγορά) doubled up as a place where goods could be bought and sold (i.e. a marketplace) and where people gathered generally for debating, election-eering and also for putting on trials. And if a member of the public wished to stand up and address his fellow citizens – that is, speak in the *agora* – the verb used to define what he was doing was *agoreuein* (ἀγορεύειν), 'to speak in public'.

If, however, the speech was being made during the course of legal proceedings the verb acquired the prefix *kata-* (κατα-), 'against', so that the new composite verb *katagoreuein* (καταγορεύειν) meant 'to speak against', or 'to accuse'. And the citizens who were at the *agora* because they were on trial or otherwise facing accusations of one sort or another were separated from those who were there just to do some shopping. That is, they were kept to one side as a group or 'category' of their own.

The word has been used in English to mean a class or division since the late sixteenth century.

## Cemetery

If we pronounce the initial 'c' as a 'k' instead of an 's' we get a good idea of the derivation of this word. It is simply the anglicized form of the Greek *koimētērion* (κοιμητήριον), which is related to two verbs: *koimaō* (κοιμάω), 'I put to sleep', and *keimai* (κεῖμαι), 'I lie'. So we could say that the basic meaning behind both the Greek and the English forms of the word is 'a place to lie down and go to sleep'.

The word was not used in English until the fourteenth century.

## Centre

'Centre' (oro 'center' in American English) has as its origin the Greek *kentron* (κέντρον), meaning 'a sharp point', 'spike' or 'goad'. The reference here is to the early Greek mathematicians, who, while they were developing what we now refer to as 'geometry', would draw circles by placing the 'sharp point' of a set of compasses where they wanted the middle or 'centre' of a circle to be. The verb from which the noun is derived is the Greek *kentein* (κέντεῖν), 'to prick' or 'to goad'. 'Centre' has been used in English since the fourteenth century.

# Chair

In the thirteenth century the Old French word *cheare* or *cheier* overtook the original Old English term *stol* (modern English 'stool') as the term used to define the article of furniture designed to allow people sit down to rest.

The French term was a considerably modified form of the Latin *cathedra*, an easy chair, mainly used by women. This was adopted from the Greek *kathedra* (καθέδρα), a combination of *kata* (κατὰ), 'down', and *hedra* (ἕδρα), 'seat' or 'bench'; the associated verb was *kathēsthai* (καθῆσθαι), 'to sit down'. And *kathedra* is the origin of the word 'cathedral', which is, of course, a religious building where, traditionally, a bishop has his 'seat'.

# Charisma

Anyone described as having 'charisma' is usually thought of as being blessed with personal traits and characteristics endowing them with a certain magnetism which the rest of us lack. It is a direct borrowing from the Greek *charisma* (χάρισμα), 'grace' or 'favour', and has been used by the Christian Church since the seventeenth century to mean 'a free gift of God's grace'; it is derived from the noun *charis* (χάρις), meaning 'loveliness', 'physical grace' and 'charm'. But it was also used to describe the feelings of kindness and goodwill in those displaying sympathetic concern to others, as well as the sense of gratitude felt by those who benefited from such kindness.

### THE CHARITIES OR GRACES

Most people in the modern world are aware of the Three
Graces because of the delightful sculpture originally
created in 1814 (there were several versions) by Antonio
Canova and now housed in the Hermitage Museum, St
Petersburg. They were originally goddesses from Greek
mythology who conferred grace and charm on any social
gathering and even had the power to bring victory to
chosen competitors in the games. They were:

| | |
|---|---|
| *Aglaia* | Splendour |
| *Euphrosunē* | Mirth |
| *Thalia* | Good cheer and the bloom of youth. |

They were usually considered to be the daughters of Zeus
and Eurynome, although some sources name Dionysos
and Aphrodite as their parents.

## Chemist

If we think of a chemist as basically a man or woman who
pours concoctions of one sort or another from one bowl
into another, we are well on the way to understanding
the origin of the word.

The immediate antecedent of the word is probably the
Arabic *alkhimia*, the origin of the Middle English word
'alchemy', a science whose adherents, in the Middle Ages,
spent their days trying to convert base metal into gold

or silver. But the Arabic is derived ultimately from the Greek verb *chein* (χεῖν), 'to pour', which is related to words such as *chutra* (χύτρα), 'pot' or 'jar', and *chumos* (χυμός), 'liquid' or 'juice'. And the Greek term for 'chemistry' was either *chumeia* (χυμεία) or *chumikē technē* (χυμική τέχνη), the latter meaning, quite literally, 'the art of pouring'.

The terms 'chemist' and 'chemistry' have been used in English since the early seventeenth century.


## Chimney

The most primitive kind of chimney was nothing more than a hole in the roof, strategically placed to let out the smoke rising from a fire in the centre of the room. As architecture became more refined, people found more skilful ways of dispelling the smoke and by the fourteenth century chimneys, as we would recognize them today, began to appear in castles, manor houses and even the dwellings of the poor. But they were not a common feature of houses in Britain until the sixteenth or seventeenth century.

The word 'chimney' itself was borrowed in the fourteenth century from the Old French *cheminée*, originally meaning either the device for conducting the smoke away from the living areas or a room in which a *cheminée* was situated. The French word was a borrowing of the Late Latin *caminata*, an adjective from the noun *caminus*, 'furnace', 'forge', which was probably part of the expression *camera caminata*, 'a room with a furnace'. And the Latin *caminus* was taken from the Greek *kaminos* (κάμῑνος), 'oven', 'furnace' or 'kiln'.

But there is more to the story. The original furnaces would probably have had a curved or arched covering designed to guide the smoke away from the fire beneath. This arched covering was known in Greek as a *kamara* (καμάρα), the origin not only of 'chimney' but also of 'chamber', originally a room with a chimney or hearth in it.


## Chiropodist

When the word was first used in English in the eighteenth century it applied to doctors who specialized in treating problems of the hands and feet; nowadays such medical practitioners have forgotten about the hands and concentrate solely on the feet. In fact, since the early twentieth century the original term has been replaced by the more accurate 'podiatrist', combining the Greek for foot with *iatros* (ἰατρός), 'doctor'.

The original word is thought to have been coined by a Canadian doctor (with the very appropriate name of Daniel Palmer) who combined the Greek for 'hand' and 'foot', *cheir* (χείρ) and *pous* (πούς), and, with a little manipulation, produced 'cheiropodist', which later changed to our present-day spelling.

## Chronic

Overuse of this word has meant that it has lost much of its original meaning. It tends to be used now in certain circles as a synonym for 'serious' or even, colloquially, for 'bad'. The origin of the word, however, is simply the Greek for 'time', *chronos* (χρόνος), and its associated adjective *chronios* (χρόνιος), meaning 'long lasting'. A 'chronic' medical condition is really one that is persistent rather than serious or life-threatening.

'Chronic' entered English in the fifteenth century. Other associated words include 'chronometer' (a watch or timepiece), 'chronology' (timescale) and 'anachronism' (the attribution of an event, custom or artefact to the wrong historical time).

*ho chronos eumarēs theos*

ὁ χρόνος εὐμαρής θεός

'Time is a kindly god'

SOPHOCLES, *ELEKTRA*

## Church

The best clue to the origin of this word is actually the Scots term 'kirk', as it retains the 'k' sound reflected in the Greek spelling. Medieval Greek had the combination *kuriakon dōma* (χυριαχόν δῶμα), meaning quite literally 'the Lord's house', from the noun *kurios* (κύριος), 'lord', 'master' or, strictly speaking, 'one who holds *kuros*' (κύρος), supreme power. The full Greek term was abbreviated to *kuriakon* (κυριακόν), 'belonging to the lord'; by the time the word made its way into Old English it was written *cirice* but pronounced 'chiriche'. This eventually evolved into the pronunciation we recognize today.

The Greek noun *dōma* (δῶμα), 'dwelling', is derived from the verb *demein* (δέμειν), 'to build', and both noun and verb are the source (via the Latin *domesticus*) of the English adjective 'domestic'.


# Cinema

In the USA what we normally refer to as a cinema is known as a 'movie theatre' or simply 'the movies'. It has to be admitted that the Americans are closer to the etymological origins of the word than the British are.

'Cinema' is taken directly from the Greek *kinein* (κινεῖν), 'to move', and the plural noun *kinēmata* (κινήματα), 'moving things'. The term was devised by the nineteenth-century pioneers in the field of film-making, who were merely following the fashion of the day to give all technological and/or scientific innovations definitions coined from the Greek.

Many cinemas and theatres around the world take their names from the Greek. They include:

| | |
|---|---|
| *Adelphi* | literally, 'the brothers' |
| *Apollo* | Greek god of music, poetry, art and so on |
| *Criterion* | Greek for 'the standard' |
| *Lyceum* | from *lukeion* (λύχειον), an Athenian garden |
| *Lyric* | named after poets who sang accompanied by the lyre |
| *Atlas* | in Greek mythology, the Titan who held up the Earth |
| *Odeon* | literally, a place 'for singing' |
| *Hippodrome* | a place where 'horses run' |

## Clematis

Probably one of the most popular garden plants through-out Europe, if not the world, the clematis has been confused historically and linguistically with other plants we generally refer to as 'climbers'.

The name 'clematis' was first recorded in English in the 1550s, although it appears to have been adopted from the Latin *clematis* as an alternative name for the plant known in Britain since Anglo-Saxon times and colloquially referred to as the 'periwinkle'.

The Latin *clematis* was a direct borrowing of the Greek *klēmatis* (χληματίς), a 'creeping plant', although the noun from which *klēmatis* was derived had nothing to do with creeping or crawling. A *klēma* (χλῆμα) could be either a shoot or a twig broken off a branch and then used as a cutting to be grafted onto another tree. This practice was particularly common among farmers growing and tending the vines that went on to produce the wines for which parts of Ancient Greece were famous. Possibly the tendency for both the clematis and the vine to twist and turn has contributed to the botanical and the etymological confusion.

If we return to the periwinkle we see that the associations with twisting and twining are reinforced. The Old English name was *perwince*, the Middle English was *perwince* and both were allied to the Latin verb *vincire*, 'to bind', 'to wind', and *pervincire*, 'to bind excessively'.

## Clinic

In modern Britain, if we are feeling ill we have a choice of places we can go in order to seek medical attention. We can go to our GP's surgery, to a hospital, or we might nip down to a local clinic – a usage which illustrates the reversal in the meaning associated with this word.

It came into English as a borrowing from the French *clinique* in the 1620s. The French had acquired it from the Latin *clinicus*, who in ancient Rome was a physician who would visit patients lying in bed because they were, presumably, too ill to walk to wherever the physician held his surgery. Even in seventeenth-century English the word 'clinic' referred to the patient lying prostrate in his or her bed rather than the place where medical attention was available to those in need of it.

The Latin noun was taken directly from the Greek *klinē* (χλίνη), 'bed', and the concept of the *klinikē technē* (χλινιχή τέχνη), literally 'bed skill', best translated perhaps as 'bedside manner'. And behind the noun was the verb *klinein* (χλίνειν), 'to put into a leaning or lying position'.

## ARISTOPHANĒS

Very little is known about the early life of Aristophanēs. The estimates of his date of birth differ considerably: some authorities say he was born *c.*444 BCE on the island of Aegina, but we cannot be sure. He is thought to have written forty plays, although only eleven of them have survived. These, however, are extremely important for the historian as they contain many descriptions of the prominent men of the day and provide an invaluable insight into the structure and mechanism of contemporary Athenian society. He is also admired among classicists for the purity of his Attic Greek and his exemplary skill in its use.

Aristophanes satirized the 'new thinking' of Socrates in *The Clouds* (423 BCE); demonstrated the power of women willing to withdraw their sexual favours until their demands are met in *Lysistrata* (411 BCE); and in *The Wasps* (422 BCE) attacked the increasingly litigious society emerging in the Athens of the day. His other plays include *The Frogs* (405 BCE) and *The Birds* (414 BCE).

## Cloud cuckoo land

Anyone said to live here is thought of as not being in touch with reality and of harbouring overly optimistic beliefs and convictions. It is a direct translation of the Greek *nephelokokkugia* (νεφελοκοκκυγία), made up from three words: *nephelē* (νεφέλη), 'cloud', *kokkuks* (κόκκυξ), 'cuckoo', and *gē* (γῆ), 'land'.

The person responsible for the term was *Aristophanēs* (Ἀριστοφάνης), an Athenian playwright whose play *hoi Ornithes* (οἱ Ὄρνιθες), *The Birds*, envisages constructing a 'cloud cuckoo land' between Heaven and Earth where the inhabitants would be able to interrupt all communication between man and the gods.


## Coffin

The object we now refer to as a 'coffin', a box designed specifically as a receptacle for our bones when we cast off our mortal coil, has only had this meaning since the early sixteenth century.

Prior to that the word had a much more general meaning, and in the fourteenth century designated a chest or box in which jewellery and other valuables were kept, much the same as did the related thirteenth-century word 'coffer'. In the late fourteenth century it was also the term for piecrust surrounding dainty morsels of meat or fruit filling.

In all senses, the ultimate derivation of the word is the Greek *kophinos* (κόφινος), a universal term for any kind of basket.

## Comedy

This is a composite word, closely linked to three Greek nouns. The first is *kōmē* (κώμη), 'village', and the second is its derivative *kōmos* (κῶμος), a village revelry, carousal. No doubt these rural binges, once a certain amount of liquid refreshment had been taken, combined the laughter and bonhomie with a bit of a sing-song. And the Greek for a song, *ōdē* (ᾠδή), combined with the word for revelry to produce *kōmōdia* (κωμῳδία), a light-hearted amusing stage act. By the seventeenth century this word had been adopted into English as 'comedy'.

## Contemplate

The Greek verb *temnein* (τέμνειν), 'to cut', produced the noun *temenos* (τέμενος), an area of land 'cut off' from a larger one and suitable for quiet reflection and meditation. Eventually, such a patch of land was used for the erection of a building dedicated to the worship of a god (or gods); the Romans, adapting the Greek term, referred to such a hallowed construction as a *templum*, the origin of 'temple' in English. Therefore, 'to contemplate' when it first appeared in English in the sixteenth century meant nothing more than to meditate on a piece of land 'cut off' and set aside for the purpose.

Interestingly, another common English verb expressing a similar idea is 'consider'; this may be derived from the Latin *sidus*, 'star', and originally meant simply 'to observe the stars'. No doubt the calm thoughtfulness induced by such an activity is responsible for the meaning we attach to the word today.

## Cosmetics

The Greek word *kosmos* (κόσμος) meant 'order' and was the term for the perfect arrangement of the universe as opposed to the *chaos* (χαός) or 'chaos' that existed, so the Ancient Greeks believed, before the world began. And their concept of 'beauty', whether applied to the stars or a human being, was inseparable from their idea of order; disorder to them could never be described as beautiful. So, etymologically speaking, when someone applies lipstick and mascara, they are not so much making themselves more beautiful as simply restoring 'order'.

There is an isolated case of this word in English in the twelfth century, but it was not widely used until the seventeenth.

## Crater

Now used in English mainly to denote a depression of some sort in the Earth's surface or a feature of the surface of the Moon, the original meaning of the word was simply 'a bowl'. It entered English in the early seventeenth century as a borrowing from the Latin *crater*, adopted by the Romans from the Greek *kratēr* (κρατήρ), a bowl used mainly for mixing wine with water (the Greeks thought that only barbarians drank wine neat). The derivative verb was *kerannunai* (κεράννυναι), 'to mix', which also produced the noun *keramos* (κέραμος), 'potter's clay'. This is the origin of the adjective 'ceramic'.

## Crisis

When things are getting serious or even desperate we are usually told that there is a crisis and that something has to be done fairly soon if dreadful consequences are to be avoided. Originally, however, things were not quite so dramatic, as the word is derived from the Greek *krinein* (κρίνειν), meaning, among other things, 'to judge', 'to make a decision'. So, a 'crisis' was originally nothing more than a point in time when somebody had to make a decision about what to do next.

When the word entered English in the fifteenth century it was a medical term denoting a turning point in a disease. It was not used for the decisive point in a chain of events until the seventeenth century.

Another related word, taken directly from the Greek, is *kritērion* (κριτήριον), 'criterion', a standard by which results, conditions and so on can be measured or 'judged'.


## *Crystal*

This is a word that usually conjures up images of glistening clarity and the pure white covering on trees and flowers in the garden on a crisp, frosty morning. And such images are a fairly accurate representation of the origin of the word.

It entered English in the Middle Ages from Old French and Latin, both of which had acquired it from the Greek *krustallos* (κρύσταλλος), 'ice', and *kruos* (κρύος), 'frost'.

These words are also the root of the prefix 'cryo', used in modern English to describe any process undertaken in conditions of extreme cold, such as 'cryosurgery' (surgery undertaken with the aid of freezing) or 'cryonics' (the gruesome practice of freezing a dead body in the hope of bringing it back to life at some time in the future).

There is also an etymological thread linking 'crystal' with 'crust'. They share an Indo-European origin, as, although a 'crust' is not necessarily cold or frozen, it always appears harder than its surroundings.

## Cube

For the Greeks, as for us, any six-sided solid figure was a cube or, as the Greeks referred to it, *kubos* (κύβος). They were definitely not the inventors of dice games, but in their version contestants always threw three 'cubes' or dice, and when all three fell with the same number of pips on top, the number was said to have been 'cubed'. The mathematical term 'cubed' applied to any number multiplied twice by itself has existed in English since the sixteenth century.

The element of chance inevitably associated with the game assumed almost metaphorical significance for the Ancient Greeks and gave rise to various expressions reminiscent of the vagaries of fate and pure chance. And if a decision on some important matter could not be resolved by discussion and the force of argument, the Ancient Greeks would often opt to *krinein en kubois* (κρίνειν ἐν κύβοις), 'judge by the dice'.

## Currant

The dried fruit has been known in Britain since about 1500 and takes its name from the Ancient Greek city of *Korinthos* (Κόρινθος), Corinth. In ancient times, Corinthian traders were renowned for their commercial expertise and one of their chief exports was a small, seedless grape which proved very popular throughout the Mediterranean.

By the time the fruit found its way into France it was referred to as *raysyns de Corouns* (modern French *raisins de Corinthe*), a term which was eventually distorted into the modern English as we recognize it today, 'currant'.

Corinth was a byword among Greeks and foreigners alike for luxury and an extravagant lifestyle. And, on a practical, down-to-earth level, Corinth is also the place where roof tiles were invented, making possible the sloping roofs with which we are so familiar today.

*ou pantos andros eis Korinthon esth' ho plous*

οὐ παντὸς ἀνδρὸς εἰς Κόρινθον ἔσθ' ὁ πλοῦς

'not everyone gets to sail to Corinth'

GREEK PROVERB

## Cynic

Since the sixteenth century, 'cynic' has been used in English to describe a person whose attitudes are tinged with doubt and a certain disdain for the opinions of

## CYNICAL PHILOSOPHY

In ancient Athens, the Cynics were a group of philosophers who shunned society and were totally dismissive of what might be described as the norms of civilized behaviour. They lived on the streets like dogs, ate like dogs and copulated wherever and whenever they felt like without homage to what most people considered acceptable conduct. Such a lifestyle offers one possible etymology of their name.

The Cynics (whose most famous member was probably Diogenes, who took the group's 'back to nature' stance a little too far by living in a barrel and going barefoot even in the depths of winter) believed in self-sufficiency, freedom to say whatever they wished (no matter how offensive to others) and a life of asceticism. They also equated happiness with mental lucidity and clarity or *atuphia*, literally, thought processes undimmed by the *tuphos* (τυφος), 'smoke', of hazy thinking, and were adamant that this could be achieved only through a life of denial. All pleasures of the flesh were to be eschewed.

The founder of the group was a man called Anthisthenes (445–365 BCE), a student of Socrates. He studied rhetoric with the master and then went on to found the Cynics' school of philosophy, teaching in a seat of learning known as the *Kunosarges* (χυνόσαργες), the building of the 'flashing white dogs'. The association is another possible explanation of the group's name.

others. In extreme cases it can describe someone with a penchant for sneering criticism.

If we take the word back to its origins, however, we see that by calling someone a cynic we are really comparing them (unfavourably, it has to be said) with a dog. It is derived from the Greek *kuōn* (κύων), 'dog'.

## Democracy

This Greek word has spread all over the world, in one form or another; some very 'undemocratic' states insist on referring to themselves as democracies. It is first recorded in English in the sixteenth century, derived, via French and Medieval Latin, from the Greek *dēmos* (δῆμος), 'country district', 'ordinary people', and, in fifth-century BCE Athens, 'citizens'. This word was combined with *kratos* (κράτος), 'power', 'rule', to give *dēmokratia* (δημοκρατία), 'rule by the citizens'.

There is, however, an unfortunate irony in the way the Athenians used the term. When they spoke of their citizens having the right to partake in political debate and have an input into discussions concerning what laws should be adopted, women and slaves were excluded. The idea of a 'democratic' state numbering slaves among its populace appears not to have occurred to them as being something of a contradiction in terms.

Here are a few more '-ocracies':

| | |
|---|---|
| *Albocracy* | government by white people |
| *Meritocracy* | government by the most qualified |
| *Ochlocracy* | government by the mob |
| *Gerontocracy* | government by old people |
| *Autocracy* | government by one person |
| *Plutocracy* | government by the rich |
| *Timocracy* | government by those who seek honours |

## Despot

When revolutions were raging across Europe in the eighteenth century the word 'despot' acquired sinister connotations which it had not previously enjoyed. During the French Revolution it was applied to those who were about to lose their heads to Madame Guillotine, as it suddenly became synonymous with 'cruel tyrant'. Previously the word had existed (in French since the fourteenth century and in English since the 1560s) as a term meaning not much more than an absolute ruler. It had been borrowed from the Medieval Latin *despota* and the original Greek *despotēs* (δεσπότης); in ancient Athens it was applied to oriental rulers, whose subjects were, almost without exception, slaves.

The original Greek word *despotēs* (δεσπότης) relates to two other words, *domos* (δόμος), 'house', and *posis* (πόσις), 'lawful husband', 'master'. The original meaning of 'despot', therefore, was really nothing more than 'head of the household'.

*heis esti doulos oikias, ho despotēs*

εἷς ἐστὶ δοῦλος οἰκίας, ὁ δεσπότης

'there's only one slave in a family,
the head of the household'

MENANDER

## Devil

Most of us think of the Devil as being the embodiment of evil who lives in Hell and spends his days trying to entrap us into joining him when we die. The derivation of the word, however, is somewhat more prosaic.

The Greek word *ballein* (βάλλειν) meant 'to throw', and when it was combined with the prefix *dia-* (δια), producing *diaballein* (διαβάλλειν), it acquired the meaning of 'to throw at'. Over time this was used to define the action of 'throwing unfounded accusations', or 'to slander'. And the associated Greek noun *diabolos* (διάβολος), 'slanderer', eventually evolved into our word 'devil'.

The word entered Old English as an epithet for the supreme spirit of evil or simply a malignant person. In the seventeenth century it acquired the additional meaning of a printer's apprentice, and by the eighteenth century its application had spread to the kitchen; a highly seasoned fried or boiled dish was frequently referred to as being 'devilled'.

## DEVIL OR DEMON?

'Demon' and 'devil' always have negative connotations in modern English. But the original Greek term *daimōn* (δαίμων) had several meanings, all of which were very positive. It could mean a god, a goddess or a deity as well as one's fate or destiny. The related plural noun *ta daimonia* referred to a race of divine beings who ranked below the top gods, *hoi theoi*, but were not as lowly as mortal men. Homer used the term *ta daimonia* to mean 'divine visitations' and Socrates referred to his *daimonion*, 'little demon', which we would probably call his 'genius' or even 'inspiration'. For Plato the *daimones* were the souls of mortals who made it possible for the living to connect with the gods. The negative interpretations associated with 'demons' were a later development reinforced by early Christians' antipathy to anything that did not fit in with their concept of how the universe is arranged or smacked of polytheism.

## *Diagnosis*

The word 'diagnosis' applies now to almost any situation where we have to find out what is wrong. Our cars can be subjected to a 'diagnostic' test; computers have built-in 'diagnostic' problem-solving programmes; and if we go to the doctor's because we are not feeling up to the mark, the doctor will examine us and make a 'diagnosis' before prescribing drugs or suggesting a course of treatment.

When the word appeared in English in the seventeenth century its use was restricted to the world of medicine. It was a borrowing of the Greek noun *diagnōsis* (διάγνωσις), which really meant a 'distinguishing between two possibilities', from the verb *diagignōskein* (διαγιγνώσκειν), 'to make a distinction'. The implication here is that when we make a diagnosis we consider the possible causes of a problem and attempt to isolate the real one.

But there is another possibility. In Athens, specifically, *diagignōskein* was a legal term meaning 'to decide', 'to make a judgement', and this could be the derivation of the word as it is used in modern English. After all, both the doctor examining us and the garage mechanic rooting about under a car bonnet have to arrive at a judgement as to what to do next.

By changing the prefix on the Greek verb from *dia-* (δια-) to *pro-* (προ-), 'before', we move to a new verb, *progignōskein* (προγιγνώσκειν), meaning 'to know beforehand'. And this is the derivation of another word used commonly in modern English, 'prognosis'.

## Dialogue

This is a direct borrowing into English of the Greek noun *dialogos* (διάλογος), meaning 'a conversation'. It is a combination of the basic verb (*legein*) (λέγειν), 'to say', and the prefix *dia-* (δια-), forming a compound verb *dialegesthai* (διαλέγεσθαι), indicating that the action of

the verb is performed 'one with another' (equating with the Latin *inter-*).

This compound verb, however, had another meaning, with implications for modern English. When two or more people are engaged in conversation, the 'conversation' not infrequently develops into a debate and then into a full-blown argument. The Greek term for the art of debate was *dialektikē technē* (διαλεκτικὴ τέχνη), and anyone who was particularly adept at, or skilled in, such argument was described as being *dialektikos* (διαλεκτικός). An associated noun was *dialektos* (διάλεκτος), a 'debate' or 'argument'. But this word also expanded its association with verbal dexterity and came to mean 'the language of a country'. In English the derivative word 'dialect' has been used since the 1570s to denote the speech of a particular area or region.

# Diet

If a doctor tells a slightly overweight patient that he or she has to go on a permanent diet, with the implication that a complete lifestyle change is necessary, he or she is not all that far from the original Greek idea. *Diaitia* (δίαιτια) meant 'a way of life', and the related verb *diaitan* (διαιτᾶν) meant 'to adopt a particular way of living'.

In the thirteenth century, when the word first appeared in English, it was simply a synonym for food. The attendant restrictions on the amount of food and alcohol to be consumed date only from the fourteenth century.

# Dilemma

Some, if not most, people tend to use this word nowadays as a convenient synonym for a difficulty or a problem, particularly if it leaves them feeling helpless and not knowing which way to turn.

The word entered English in the 1520s as a borrowing from Late Latin and ultimately Greek, which had the word *dilēmma* (δίλημμα), an argument in which an opponent was forced to make a choice between two alternatives, neither of which was desirable or even acceptable. On a more practical level, a man caught on the top of a burning building might have to choose between staying where he is and burning to death, or jumping and almost certainly being killed by the fall. This would also be a 'dilemma' as understood by the Ancient Greeks.

The Greek *dilēmma* (δίλημμα) comprises two elements: *di-* (δι-), 'two', and *lēmma* (λῆμμα), which in logic was understood as an assumption or premiss taken for granted. Its derivative verb was *lambanein* (λαμβάνειν), which had several meanings, all involving some idea of taking, accepting or receiving. When used with the meaning of an assumption or premiss, it is not all that distant from the way in which we speak of having a 'take' on a situation or discussion when we really mean an 'opinion'.

## Dinosaur

When amateur and professional archaeologists began digging up the fossils of strange animals in the nineteenth century, nobody had any idea what to call them. But then a certain Lancastrian by the name of Richard Owen combined the Greek words for 'terrible' and 'lizard', *deinos* (δεινός) and *sauros* (σαύρος), producing the composite noun 'dinosaur', meaning simply 'terrible lizard'.

Most of the dinosaurs were given names taken from Greek. Here are just a few of them:

| | |
|---|---|
| *Brontosaurus* | thunder lizard |
| *Stegosaurus* | covered lizard |
| *Brachiosaurus* | lizard with arms |
| *Diplodokos* | two-beamed lizard |
| *Megalosaurus* | great lizard |
| *Triceratops* | three-horned face |
| *Tyrannosaurus* | tyrant lizard |
| *Ankulosaurus* | stiff lizard |

# Diploma

Long before a diploma was awarded to successful candidates in an academic institution (the 1680s) it referred to a document issued by governments to their representatives as proof of identity and status while travelling in foreign climes. Also in the seventeenth century it could be an official document of either the church or the state when bestowing particular honours or privileges on the bearer. All this sounds rather grand, but the basic meaning of the word is very prosaic; it refers to nothing more than a piece of paper that had been 'folded in two'.

It entered English in the seventeenth century as a borrowing of the Latin *diploma*, from the Greek *diplōma* (δίπλωμα), a noun derived from the verb *diploun* (διπλοῦν), 'to fold', and its related adjective *diplous* (διπλοῦς), 'folded in two'.

Another derivative noun is, of course, 'diplomat'; once again, the highly elevated position occupied by such a person in government circles appears somewhat exaggerated when compared to the origin of the term. We think of a 'diplomat' as a highly educated person who possesses rare personal skills and can be relied upon to deal with foreign governments in perhaps difficult situations. In reality, however, the title is conferred on somebody who, literally, carries 'a piece of paper folded into two'.

# Disaster

The Greeks were not alone in the ancient or modern world in believing that our lives are governed by the stars (just think how we can still 'count our lucky stars' or describe someone as being born 'under a lucky star'). It was the Italians and the French who first had the idea of resorting to Greek to compose a word suggesting an alien influence behind a terrible misfortune. They took the prefix *dus-* (δυς-), 'bad', 'unfortunate', and combined it with the noun *astēr* (ἀστήρ), 'star', adjusted the spelling a little, and coined *disastro* and *désastre* respectively. English followed suit with 'disaster', synonymous with 'calamity' in the seventeenth century.

# Disco

In 1964 the word 'disco' found its way into English as a borrowing from the Americans, who shortened the word *discothèque*, which they acquired from the French in 1954, who in turn had adopted and adapted the Italian *discoteca*. This was a word which the Italians had coined in 1932 (based on *biblioteca*, a collection of books) to define a collection of gramophone records.

The Italian *discoteca* is a combination of the Greek nouns *diskos* (δίσκος), 'a round plate', and *thēkē* (θήκη), 'a box used for storage'. The original concept behind the term was simply a place where plates or any round, flat objects could be stored for safe-keeping.

# Dish

The Anglo-Saxons referred to a plate or bowl as a *disc*; this has evolved into the word as we recognize it today. The Old English spelling is a more accurate reflection of the Latin derivative noun *discus*, borrowed in turn from the Greek *diskos* (δίσκος). This basically meant 'a quoit', but it was later applied to almost anything round and flat, such as a dinner plate or even a mirror. And it is of course the same word as 'discus', the implement used in throwing contests on the athletics field. The origin of the word is the verb *dikein* (δικεῖν), 'to throw', 'to hurl'; so, if the stories of Greeks throwing plates on the floor after a meal are true, there would appear to be a connection between the custom and the etymological derivation of the word.

And there are some interesting cognates. At some point in history it was realized that the round, flat object designed for throwing could be scaled up a little and fitted with legs to produce a table, suitable specifically for writing letters, documents, and so on – that is, 'a desk'. This term for a writing table has existed in English since the mid-fourteenth century. It is also the origin of the word 'disk' (or alternatively 'disc') in all its uses.

# Door

Few people would expect this to be anything other than a pure and simple English word, but in fact it has a long and ancient history with a rather surprising linguistic relative in the world of anatomy.

'Door' is descended from Old English *duru*, and closely related to the modern German *Tür* and *Tor* 'door' and 'gate', and the Greek *thura* (θύρα), 'door'. All can trace their origins back to the original Indo-European root *dhwer-/*dhur-, also meaning 'door'.

In the world of medicine, however, it made a surprise appearance in 1849 when the associated term 'thyroid gland' was first used in English. This was a direct translation of the Greek *chondros thureoeidēs* (χόνδρος θυρεοειδής), which could be translated as 'thyroid cartilage'. The literal meaning is, however, slightly more complicated. The related Greek noun *thureos* (θυρεός) meant both (i) a large stone placed against a door to keep it shut, and (ii) a large oblong shield.

The 'thyroid cartilage' or simple 'thyroid' was originally thought of as a 'shield-shaped' piece of cartilage 'resembling the stone in front of a door'.

The Greek term was coined by the physician Galen (*c.*130–*c.*210 CE) to describe what we colloquially refer to as the 'Adam's apple'.

## Draconian

Draconian, or particularly harsh, laws take their name from Draco, the seventh-century BCE Athenian law-giver who drew up a system of punishments for various infringements of the law. Even by the fairly brutal standards of the day, Draco's punishments were seen as excessively cruel as the most minor misdemeanours could exact the death penalty.

The name Draco (*Drakōn*/Δράκων in Greek) is almost certainly the same as *drakōn* (δράκων), the word for a serpent or giant sea fish, which has given us the word 'dragon'. 'Dragons' were so-called because they had eyes that 'gleamed' and 'flashed', the infinitive for which in Greek was *drakein* (δρακεῖν).

## Drastic

When this word first appeared in English in the late seventeenth century its use was restricted to the world of medicine and described potions that would hopefully have a powerful effect on bowel movements. The Greek adjective from which it was derived was *drastikos* (δραστικός), 'active', from the verb *dran* (δρᾶν), 'to do', and its verbal adjective *drasteon* (δραστέον), 'what has to be done'. The first use of the word in English meaning 'urgent' or 'extreme' dates from the early nineteenth century.

Interestingly, the same Greek verb produced *drama* (δρᾶμα), 'deed', 'act', 'business', as well as an 'action represented on the stage'. And this is our word 'drama' in all its meanings.

# Echo

The Greek noun *ēchē* (ἠχή) was imitative of the roar of the seas and oceans, and its associated word *ēchō* (ἠχώ) was the term for a reverberating sound such as the type we now associate with an 'echo'. But the Greeks, who interpreted everything in terms of gods and goddesses, personified the sound as *Echo* (Ἠχώ), a nymph of the mountains.

The same Greek word is at the root of the word 'catechism', which strictly speaking is a method of learning based on 'echoing' or repeating phrases as instructed by a teacher.

'Echo' was adopted into English from Greek (via Old French and Latin) in the fourteenth century.


# Economy

It is a testament to the pervasive influence Greek has had on world culture that almost every language in the world uses this word, in modified forms, to define the concern for, and management of, money and resources.

It was first used in English in the 1530s when its meaning of 'household management' reflected the sense of the original Greek word *oikonomos* (οἰκόνομος), an adjective used as a noun and meaning 'the person in charge of the management of the house'. The constituent elements are *oikos* (οἶκος), 'house', and *nomos* (νόμος), 'management', 'law'.

By the 1650s the meaning of the word had widened and it was now being applied not solely to the management of an individual dwelling, but to the country as a whole. Its relationship not with simply management but with careful spending and even frugality was a development of the 1660s.

In 1873 the German zoologist Ernst Haeckel (1834–1919) coined the word 'ecology'. This also was based on the Greek for a house, *oikos* (οἶκος), but now the word was combined with *logos* (λόγος), 'study', and the new word was designed to reflect Haeckel's study of, and concern for, the relationship between all living creatures and their global habitat. From the 1960s 'ecology' was adopted also by those who were determined to take action to put an end to, or at least reduce, those of mankind's activities which are harmful to the environment.

## Electricity

In the seventeenth century two English men of science, Sir Thomas Browne and William Gilbert, were fascinated by what appeared to be a strange force of nature which could be activated by rubbing certain substances together. They noticed also that this force was particularly strong in the case of amber; when it was rubbed vigorously it seemed to generate a force which had the ability to attract other objects. William Gilbert conducted many early experiments into magnetism and was obviously interested in this newly discovered force but needed to find a name for it. He decided to use the Late Latin *electrum*, 'like amber', itself derived from the Greek *electron* (ἤλεκτρον), which had two meanings in the world of Homer. It was either applied to amber or it was the term used by Greek metalworkers to describe a naturally occurring alloy of gold and silver, no doubt on account of its resemblance to the gleaming Sun, the Greek term for which was *ēlektōr* (ἠλέκτωρ).

## Elixir

This is a word often used in the modern world to mean little more than a liquid intended to relieve the symptoms of ailments ranging from arthritis, haemorrhoids and rheumatism to a simple cough. Historically, it featured in expressions such as 'elixir of youth' and 'elixir of life', used by those who claimed that their magic potions would bestow eternal youth or extend a person's life.

In the thirteenth century it was referred to in Medieval Latin as *elixir*, otherwise known as 'the philosopher's stone', which was credited with the ability to turn base metal into gold. By the time the word entered English in the fourteenth century it had gained the additional reputation of being able to ward off impending death.

It is thought that the word was adopted into English from the Arabic *al-iksir*, which had been acquired from the Greek. The early Greek doctors would apply a special powder renowned for its ability to dry up gaping wounds in the hope that this would aid the healing process and possibly save a life. The term they used for this powder was *ksērion* (ξήριον), a noun derived from the adjective *ksēros* (ξηρός), 'dry'.

By the 1590s an 'elixir' was a strong tonic offered to the sick in the hope that it would make them feel better, if not recover fully from whatever was ailing them. By the middle of the seventeenth century it was a general term for the concoctions peddled by quack doctors.

## Embryo

The *Oxford English Dictionary* tells us that this word entered English in the sixteenth century, but other sources suggest that it was being used in English as early as the fourteenth. Whichever is correct, it was a borrowing from the Late Latin *embryo* or *embryon*, taken from the Greek *embruon* (ἔμβρυον), a composite word made up of *em-* (ἐμ-) for *en-* (ἐν-), 'in', and the verb *bruein* (βρύειν), 'to be full', 'to swell'. The literal meaning of 'embryo', therefore, is 'something that is swelling inside'.

For the Ancient Greeks in the time of Plato and Socrates, the word *embruon* meant the same as 'embryo' now means in modern English. But for Homer, several centuries earlier, it meant a newborn lamb or kid.

# Emporium

In Ancient Greece there were two categories of shop-keeper: those who traded locally on a small scale, known as *kapēloi* (κάπηλοι), and those who travelled considerable distances in order to sell their wares. The latter group were known as *emporoi* (ἔμποροι) and they took their name from the verb *poreuesthai* (πορεύεσθαι), 'to travel', with its associated noun *poros* (πόρος), 'way', 'route'. Valiant and determined traders would travel far afield, crossing seas if necessary, frequently finding it more convenient to establish an *emporion* (ἐμπόριον) in a distant land than to keep trailing back and forth to their place of origin. And the word *emporion* (ἐμπόριον) was recorded in Latin as 'emporium', the form of the word that was adopted into English in the sixteenth century

# Energy

We all need energy. It does not matter if we are function-ing as individuals or as members of the larger society; if we have no access to energy we cease to exist. The reason we need energy is that, from the earliest days of prehistory, man has had to work in order to survive and this is a clue to the etymology of the word.

When the word first entered English in the sixteenth century it meant vigour of expression; by the seventeenth it implied the force or power a person could display; and by the nineteenth it referred to intensity of action.

The original Greek word was *energeia* (ἐνέργεια), which itself comprised *en-* (ἐν-), 'in', and *ergon* (ἔργον), 'work'. Our 'energy' is literally the capacity for work or activity 'within' each of us.

> *eudaimonia estin energeia tis tēs psuchēs*
>
> εὐδαιμονία ἐστὶν ἐνέργειά τις τῆς ψυχῆς
>
> 'happiness is an activity of the soul'
>
> ARISTOTLE

## Enigma

Anything that we find difficult to understand can be defined either as an 'enigma' or as being 'enigmatic'. The Greek idea behind the word is *ainigma* (αἴνιγμα), 'a puzzle', and the derivative verb *ainissesthai* (αἰνίσσεσθαι), 'I speak in riddles'. But both of these words evolved from the basic *ainos* (αἶνος), meaning 'a story', suggesting that the original Greek storytellers honed their art by introducing an element of surprise and a certain intellectual challenge to their tales in order to confuse or baffle their listeners.

As a riddle in verse, the word was first used in English in the sixteenth century; by the seventeenth it was being applied more widely to confusing or puzzling situations.

# Enthusiastic

This adjective has been used in English since the eighteenth century to describe anyone who demonstrates a certain passion for a particular project, enterprise or just about any other form of human activity. But the original meaning of the Greek word, from which it is derived, suggests that 'enthusiasm' is evidence that the person concerned is possessed by a god.

The two Greek words *en-* (ἐν-), 'in', and *theos* (θεός), 'god', combined to produce the adjective *entheos* (ἔνθεος), 'inspired', 'god within', and the derivative verb (*enthousiazein*) (ἐνθουσιάζειν), 'to be inspired'.

Prior to the eighteenth century anyone described as 'enthusiastic' was thought of as being in the grip of religious frenzy or displaying a groundless confidence in the power of divine inspiration.


# Epitome

This word has been used in English since the sixteenth century as an alternative to 'summary' or 'abridgement' and as such has not changed much in meaning from the original Greek, *epitomē* (ἐπιτομή), 'a cutting short'. The derivation is the verb *temnein* (τέμνειν), 'to cut', combined with the prefix *epi-* (ἐπι-), 'on', to give *epitemnein* (ἐπιτέμνειν), 'to cut the surface of'. The original meaning, therefore, of an 'epitome' of a report or account appears to have been the concept of 'detaching the top' (the most important part) and ignoring, or at least giving less prominence to, the remaining comparatively minor details.

## *Ethical*

This adjective has made a long journey from its origins in Ancient Greek. The Greek noun *ēthos* (ἦθος) meant nothing more than an 'accustomed place'. In the plural, *ēthea* (ἤθεα) was a term used to define the haunts of wild animals but over time it came to be applied also to the homes and dwellings of human beings.

Of course, when people gather together regularly in specified places, certain norms of behaviour have to be adhered to if the emerging social group is to survive in an atmosphere of peace and harmony. This gave rise to the secondary meaning of the word: disposition, temper, character. An 'ethical' attitude was required from all the individual members and they had to conduct themselves in what the majority considered a morally acceptable manner. To the Greeks this meant that certain standards of behaviour had to be worked out and agreed upon, which led to the group's 'ethical philosophy' or *ēthikē philosophia* (ἠθική φιλοσοφία).

This concept was expressed in Late Latin as *ethica*; by the thirteenth century it had appeared in French as *étique*, usually translated as 'moral philosophy'. In the late fourteenth century it was adopted into English as *ethic*, 'the study of morals'. By the very early seventeenth century the adjective 'ethical' had appeared with more or less the meaning we attach to it today, 'pertaining to morality'.

## Euphoria

Synonymous with feelings of extreme happiness or elation, 'euphoria' has only had this meaning in English since the end of the nineteenth century. In the eighteenth century it was a medical term applied by doctors or physicians to a patient's condition if he or she was feeling healthy and able to withstand the rigours of everyday life. And this is a clue to the derivation of the word.

The Greek prefix *eu-* (εὖ-), 'well', 'easily', combined with a derivative of the verb *pherein* (φέρειν), 'to carry', 'to bear', to form the adjective *euphoros* (εὔφορος), 'well or patiently borne'. And if the same adjective was applied to a person, it signified that he or she was of sound, healthy body.

It would appear, therefore, that the meaning we attach to the word today has changed a little. If we are now feeling 'euphoric' the likelihood is that we feel as though we are being carried away by feelings of joy and happiness.

## Eureka

It has now become almost de rigueur to talk about having a 'eureka moment' if the answer to a knotty problem suddenly dawns on us. For an explanation of why we should use this particular exclamation of surprise, delight and satisfaction, we need to have a brief look at Greek grammar.

In fact, the word is really *heurēka* (εὕρηκα). It is the perfect tense of the verb *heuriskein* (εὑρίσκειν), 'to find', and therefore means 'I have found [it]!'

ARCHIMEDES

The reason 'eureka' has entered the English language is supposedly due to the brilliant Athenian mathematician and scientist Archimedes (*c.*287–212 BCE). The story goes that he was asked to find out if the goldsmiths working on a crown for the king of Syracuse, Hiero II, had added base metal to the gold and were therefore short-changing the ruler and his court. Archimedes, it is said, whilst languishing in the bath one day, noticed how his body caused the water to rise further up the side of the bath the deeper he lowered himself into it. That is, he discovered what we now refer to as 'displacement' and was able to use the finding as the basis for calculating the ratio of gold to metal in the crown. He was so elated at what he had discovered that, like the archetypal absent-minded professor, he jumped out of the bath and ran naked through the streets shouting *'eureka!' 'eureka!'* – 'I've found it! I've found it!' – to the bemused (and no doubt amused) bystanders.

## Euthanasia

Now used in English exclusively to mean 'mercy killing', this word always implies that somebody has taken it upon himself or herself to end another person's life and simultaneously their suffering. But it has only had this meaning since the second half of the nineteenth century; its original meaning was 'noble' or 'good death'.

Arguably the most famous example of a 'noble death' is provided by the Greek philosopher Socrates, who, after being found guilty of 'corrupting the young' by encouraging them to question the traditional ideas concerning the gods, was condemned to death by an Athenian jury. The means of execution in those days was by poison, and Socrates duly drank the proffered cup of hemlock and died. He accepted his fate with honourable, dignified stoicism, but the manner of his going is still more akin to what we would think of as suicide than to 'euthanasia'.

The original Greek word was *euthanasia* (εὐθανασία), derived from two elements: *eu–* (εὐ-), 'well' or 'good', and *thanatos* (θάνατος), 'death'.

# Frenzy

Words such as 'frenzy', 'frantic' and 'phrenetic' are all basically variations of the same word. They came into English in the fourteenth century as borrowings of the French *frénétique*, and all suggested some sort of temporary or permanent mental derangement. The French word was derived from the Latin *phrenesis*, borrowed in turn from the Greek *phrenitis* (φρενῖτις), 'inflammation of the brain'.

The surprising thing is, however, that the Greek noun from which all these words are derived did not originally mean 'brain'. The word *phrēn* (φρήν) was often used in its plural form *phrenes* (φρένες) and was the Ancient Greek term for what we would now refer to as the 'midriff'. For Homer the word signified the heart together with the surrounding flesh and muscle, which in those days were thought to be the seat of all emotions and passions. By extension, for Homer the *phrenes* (φρένες) were the seat of life, or life itself, and stood in sharp contrast to the *psuchē* (ψῡχή) or *psyche*, the departed soul.

As the word was considered to be closely related to the heart and the emotions, it was merely a matter of time before it was used to include the mind, understanding and reason. And when the mind or the heart or the emotions were disturbed in any way, suitable nouns and adjectives were devised to describe mental imbalance, which we still use today.

Another associated word which made its way into English in the nineteenth century was 'phrenology'. According to the proponents of the theory, the lumps and bumps on a person's head were a reliable indication of his or her character, but it was fairly soon debunked and consigned to the rubbish tip along with several other pseudo-scientific ideas of the day.

## Galaxy

The word 'galaxy' has come to us from the Greek word *gala* (γάλα), meaning 'milk', because the Ancient Greeks thought that the clusters of stars they observed in the sky resembled flowing milk. In fact, the Ancient Greeks were so convinced that it was milk that the explanation of how it got there is embedded in their mythology. The goddess *Hera* (Ἥρα), Zeus' wife, was tricked into suckling the dragon guarding the Apples of the Hesperides. When she realized what was happening she tore the dragon away from her breast and the drops of milk that were spilt became the stars in the galaxy. And let's not forget that our 'galaxy' is also known as the Milky Way.

But there is an even more surprising connection here: the word 'milk'. The word entered English from the Germanic root *melg*, cognate with the Greek verb *amelgein* (ἀμέλγειν), which had several meanings. It defined primarily the act of 'squeezing' or 'pressing out', an obvious reference to the milkmaid's skill in expressing the milk from the cows' udders, but it also came to specifically mean 'to milk'. And yet another subsequent meaning was 'to sip', completing the linguistic cycle from 'squeezing', then 'milking' and finally drinking the product of all that finger action.

## Giant

It wasn't until the sixteenth century that the word 'giant' was used in English to describe people of extraordinary size. Prior to that the word was known but restricted in use to discussions of hideous, mythical monsters who bore only a passing resemblance to human beings.

WHO WERE THE GIANTS?

According to one version of the myth, Gaia gave birth to the giants after the Battle of the Titans. She did so mainly to avenge herself on the gods for locking up her children in Tartarus, the dungeon of Hades, a place of terrible torment. With the connivance of Gaia, the giants attacked the gods in what came to be known as the Battle of the Giants. The result was mayhem and destruction over all the Earth; mountains crumbled, rivers altered course and the seas flooded huge swathes of the land. This angered the gods so much that they destroyed the giants and became masters of the Earth with dominion over all its creatures.

The Greek word from which it is derived had its roots in the very earliest stages of the language. According to the poet Hesiod, the giants were the sons of *gaia* (γαῖα) or *gē* (γῆ), the mythological personification of the Earth, who provided the etymology of the word *gigas* (γίγας) and its plural *gigantes* (γίγαντες).

## Glamour

Believe it or not, the glamorous model in a fashion magazine is linguistically linked directly to the Ancient Greek verb *graphein* (γράφειν), 'to write', and the plural noun *grammata* (γράμματα), 'things written', the derivation of the English word 'grammar'.

'Glamour' first entered English in about 1720 as a Scots corruption of the word 'grammar'. We now think of this as a set of rules defining how we should construct sentences so that the end product is clearly understood by all who hear or read it, but in the eighteenth century writing was still regarded as something of an occult science. And the learned men and women who studied and mastered it were deemed to be in possession of magical powers. Indeed, an older expression for 'to cast a spell on' was 'to cast a glamour over', just as a beautiful or 'glamorous' woman is perfectly capable of leaving those around her 'spellbound'.

## Glaucoma

This potentially serious eye condition takes its name from the Greek *glaukos* (γλαυκός), which described the bluish-grey tinge observed in the pupils of those affected by the problem. The adjective is derived from the Greek for an owl, *glauks* (γλαύξ), a bird with eyes reputedly similar in colour to those of glaucoma sufferers.

There is also an interesting linguistic connection here. Athens was, and is still, famous for its teeming owl population, so when a Greek talks about *glauk' Athēnaze* (γλαῦκ' Ἀθήναζε), 'owls to Athens', he is expressing the same sentiment as we are when we talk about 'coals to Newcastle'.

The word was first used in English in the seventeenth century.

## Governor

In modern English a 'governor' is usually the chief admin-
istrator of some land-based organization. This meaning of
the word has come to us from Latin *gubernator*, but the
Romans borrowed the term from the Greek *kubernētēs*
(κυβερνήτης), originally a nautical term meaning 'helms-
man'. The idea that a leader, guiding a nation through
difficult times, is comparable to the person responsible
for steering a ship safely through choppy seas fits in well
with the concept of 'the ship of state'.

The word 'governor' entered English in the thirteenth
century.


## Greek

Most of the world refers (with slight variations in spelling)
to the country as Greece and its inhabitants as Greeks.
The Greeks, however, call themselves Hellenes and their
country Hellas. For an explanation of this confusion we
have to consider the history not only of Ancient Greece
but also of southern Italy.

For the poet Homer the *Hellēnes* (Ἕλληνες) were the
inhabitants of *Hellas* (Ἑλλάς) in Thessaly, a remote area of
what we should now refer to as northern Greece. A couple
of hundred years later Aristotle used the term *Graikoi*
(Γραικοί), claiming it was a term used by the Illyrians
and Dorians. The most likely explanation, however, is
the association with *Graia* (Γραῖα), a town on the coast of

Boeotia. At some point in the distant past migrants from Graia sailed over to southern Italy where they established settlements and made their first contacts with the locals. When the natives discovered that their new neighbours came from Graia and called themselves *graikoi* (γραικοί), they assumed that Graia was the whole country, not just an isolated part of it. So it would seem that 'Greece' and the 'Greeks' are terms for which we have to thank the people of such areas as modern Calabria, Apulia and Sicily.

### ANOTHER POSSIBILITY?

There is a tale in Greek mythology which goes as follows. The god Zeus was annoyed at the way mankind had been behaving and decided that the only thing he could do to teach them a lesson was to destroy them. His chosen method of mass annihilation was a flood which would engulf the whole Earth and drown every man, woman and child, thus ridding the world of evil.

But he did not realize that a certain Prometheus had warned his son Deucalion of Zeus' plan and advised him to take evasive action, which he promptly did. He and his wife built an ark and loaded it with sufficient provisions to last them until the waters subsided. After nine days the ark came to rest on the top of a mountain and Deucalion and his wife Pyrrha opened the door and stepped out onto dry land.

They realized that they were now the only people in the world and begged Zeus to forgive them for using trickery to evade the fate that would otherwise have awaited them. He did so and decided to make the fortunate couple the progenitors of the new breed of mankind. He now ordered them to pick up a few stones and hurl them over their shoulders, taking great care not to look behind them. The stones thrown by Deucalion became men and those thrown by Pyrrha became women; presumably the 'new' humans then paired up and went forth and multiplied so that the Earth could be populated anew.

But there is more to the story. Deucalion and his wife eventually had a family of their own (begotten by a more conventional method), the eldest of which was their son Hellen, who, according to the legend, became the father of all 'Greeks', which is why they refer to themselves as 'Hellenes'.

Do elements of this story sound vaguely familiar?

## Guitar

In Greek mythology the god Apollo was thought of as the patron of all things cultural, in particular poetry and music. He was also depicted as something of a musician himself, his instrument of choice being the *kithara* (κιθάρα), translated variously as lute, harp and lyre depending, no doubt, on the context.

When the word entered European languages, it settled down and was applied to a specific instrument, known in Latin as a *cithera*, in Old French as a *guiterre* and in Spanish as a *guitarra*. In the seventeenth century it entered English as 'guitar', a term for an instrument resembling more of what we would think of as a lute. Then, towards the end of the century, the instrument's shape and appearance began to evolve into the one we recognize today.

The first syllable of *kithara* (κιθάρα) also produced 'kit', a small fiddle, the favoured instrument of dancing masters in the early sixteenth century.

# Gym

'Gym' is now understood to be an abbreviation of 'gymnasium', as if this were the original full form of the word. In fact, 'gymnasium' is the Latin version of the Greek *gumnasion* (γυμνάσιον). And this noun is derived from the adjective *gumnos* (γυμνός), 'naked', as in Ancient Greece anyone who trained or took part in sporting contests in such an establishment did so in the nude. The word 'gymnasium' entered English in the sixteenth century.

Interestingly, in some countries the word has evolved even further. For example, in Germany a *Gymnasium* is the equivalent of a traditional grammar school in Britain and a high school in the USA.

# Halcyon

People of a nostalgic disposition often talk about the 'halcyon days' when the world was a different place and the worries of today had not yet darkened the horizon. But what some may not realize, as they reminisce about the 'good old days', is that they are recalling an Ancient Greek myth closely connected with a bird, the kingfisher.

'Halcyon days' is a direct translation of the Greek expression *halkuonides hēmerai* (ἀλκυονίδες ἡμέραι), the adjective comprising *hals* (ἅλς), 'sea', and *kuein* (κύειν), 'to conceive'. The composite noun *halkuōn* (ἀλκυών) was the Greek name for the bird we know as a 'kingfisher' and the 'halcyon days' were a couple of weeks around the winter solstice when people believed the birds calmed the weather so that they could build their nests on the sea.

The word is first recorded in English in the fourteenth century.

HALCYONE

According to the myth Halcyone was the loving and devoted wife of Ceyx, son of the Morning Star. Ceyx was involved in a shipwreck and drowned, whereupon Halcyone was so distraught that she threw herself into the sea in the hope of finding her beloved husband and spending eternity with him in the next world. But the gods were moved by the tragic events and rescued them from a watery grave, bringing the couple back up to the surface, where they changed them into kingfishers.

## HOMER

Not much is known for certain about Homer, but according to most traditions he was a blind poet or storyteller who was responsible for the epic poems the *Iliad* and the *Odyssey*. These were basically long tales based on earlier stories passed down orally from generation to generation and dealing with the war with Troy in the twelfth century BCE. The *Iliad* takes its name from *Ilion* (Ἴλιον), the Greek for Troy, and the *Odyssey* tells of the wanderings and exploits of Odysseus.

Most authorities place Homer's birth at around 700 BCE but estimates vary considerably, as do the theories about his birthplace. Because he appears to have used the Ionian dialect in his tales, some authorities assume Ionia must have been his birthplace, but others maintain that it was Chios. All that can be said about him with confidence is that his influence on the whole of European culture, particularly literature, was profound.

## *Hallucinate*

Anyone suffering from 'hallucinations' sees things that don't exist; his or her mind is 'wandering' away from reality, as the result of either extreme psychosis or mind-disturbing drugs. The word can be traced back to around 700 BCE when Homer used the noun *alē* (ἄλη), 'wandering', and the verb *alasthai* (ἀλᾶσθαι), 'to wander', 'to stray'. Both the noun and the verb acquired a more figurative meaning, associated with a distraught mind detaching itself from the real world and roaming aimlessly through life.

Strictly speaking, the word should really be 'allucinate' as there was no 'h' sound in the original Greek. It appears that the Greek word was adopted into Latin as *alucinatio* with an associated verb *alucinari*. For some unexplained reason an initial 'h' was added at a later date. This produced the noun *hallucinatio* and the spelling on which the English word was based when it was adopted in the seventeenth century.

# *Halo*

The original halos had absolutely nothing to do with religion. In fact, they have their roots among the peasants of Ancient Greece, who slaved away all day to gather the wheat which was then threshed to produce the flour that constituted a basic, staple food of the community: bread. The 'threshing floor' where this operation was carried out was known in Greek as a *halōs* (ἄλως); because of its circular shape, it came to be associated with the Sun and the Moon.

The word was adopted into English in the sixteenth century to describe the circle of light surrounding the Sun; its use as a symbol of divine light surrounding a saint's head dates from the seventeenth century.

Its figurative use, as in phrases such as 'your halo is slipping', dates from as recently as the nineteenth century.

## Harmony

There is a direct etymological link between a modern philharmonic orchestra and a carpenter in ancient Athens, toiling away to make sure the product of his labours did not fall apart as soon as it left the workshop. The verb the Athenian joiner would have had uppermost in his mind at all times was *harmozein* (ἁρμόζειν), meaning 'to fit together', 'to fit well', and he would have striven constantly to make sure that the various parts of his tables and chairs did just that.

The concept of 'fitting together' did not, however, remain the sole preserve of carpenters for long. It was soon applied to other areas of human activity where an agreement of the constituent elements was vital for the successful operation of the whole, so that the word came to define agreement or concord in almost any context. And this included the world of music where the noun *harmonia* (ἁρμονία) indicated that a particular combination of sounds had been achieved in such a way as to guarantee that the overall effect was pleasing to the ear. And another, related plural noun, *harmonika* (ἁρμονικά), in ancient Athens was the equivalent of what we now refer to as 'the theory of music' or 'music theory'.

The Greek word was adopted by the Romans as *harmonia* and then by the French with their *harmonie*, until it was adopted into English in the fourteenth century as 'harmony'.

In 1813 a society was formed in London for the promotion of instrumental music known as the Philharmonic Society of London. This took its name from a combination of the word 'harmony' with another Greek verb, *philein* (φιλεῖν), 'to love', and provided the name by which many orchestras around the world, formed to give pleasure to 'lovers of harmonious music', are known.

## Helicopter

History is littered with examples of failed attempts to get humans off the ground vertically by mechanical means. The ancient Chinese are known to have played with the idea; Leonardo da Vinci drew diagrams of fantastic machines bearing an uncanny resemblance to modern helicopters; and the eighteenth century Russian scientist Lomonosov was also fascinated by the possibilities of vertical flight. But the dreams (dare I say 'flights of fancy?')

## THE HIGH-FLYER

Greek mythology tells the story of a certain Daidalos (Latinized as Daedalus), who built the famous labyrinth on Crete but then found himself imprisoned there with his son Ikaros (Latinized as Icarus) for providing the ball of string (according to one version of the myth) which helped Theseus find his way out of the labyrinth.

Daidalos and Ikaros decided that they would escape by flying away from the island. In order to do so, Daidalos fashioned two pairs of wings, one pair for each of them, out of wax and feathers. He then warned his son not to fly too low, or the sea would wet the feathers and he would not be able to gain height. On the other hand, he also warned him that if he flew too high the heat from the Sun would melt the wax and he would plunge into the sea.

Ikaros ignored his father's wise words and soared as high as his newly acquired wings would carry him. As his father had predicted, the Sun's rays proved too much for the wax, which just melted away causing the wings to come apart. Ikaros fell from a great height and disappeared beneath the waves of what is now known as the Icarian Sea, to the south-west of the island of Samos.

The tale of Ikaros has become an oft-repeated theme in world literature and has been the subject matter of many works of art. It has also been interpreted as a warning against excessive pride and the dangers of over-ambition, as well as the need to listen to good advice.

of these early men of vision never progressed beyond the theoretical stage. Then, in the nineteenth century, the French inventor Gustave de Ponton d'Amécourt constructed a model of a prototype, but unfortunately this never progressed beyond the experimental stage either. Gustave was successful in one respect, however: in 1861, he coined the word *hélicoptère*, which was adopted, with modified spellings, into several languages in the 1920s when the first vertical flight machines were developed.

*Hélicoptère* was composed from two Greek words: *helix* (ἕλιξ), from the verb *helissein* (ἑλίσσειν), 'to twist', which was applied to almost anything with a natural tendency to curl, such as the tendril of a vine, a whirlwind or a lock of hair; and the noun *pteron* (πτερόν), a feather or, by extension, any winged creature. The French inventor had obviously understood that, had his machine taken off, its rotor blades or 'wings' would have traced a pattern in the air resembling an enormous corkscrew or ringlet.

## Helium

The chemical element we know as helium was only detected in the solar spectrum during the eclipse of the Sun which took place on 18 August 1868. The name for the new element was coined by an English astronomer Sir Joseph Lockyer and the chemist Sir Edward Frankland; they formed the word from the Greek *helios* (ἥλιος), the Sun.

But this was not the first time the Greek word had come to the aid of scientists wanting to name a new discovery. A century earlier it had been adopted in the world of botany to define the flowers that turn naturally to face the Sun, the 'heliotrope', a combination of *helios* and *tropos* (τρόπος), 'turning'. This time, however, the word was a direct borrowing and not one coined by a scientist searching for a new definition. *Heliotropion* (ἡλιοτρόπιον) was the Ancient Greeks' term for both a flower that turned towards the Sun and what we would refer to as a sundial.

## HELIOS

To the Ancient Greeks the Sun was simultaneously a god and a gigantic eye high up in the sky looking down on the mere mortals below. He was personified as Helios, the light of the Sun and the offspring of the Titans Hyperion and Theia; in the works of Homer he was the brother of Eos, 'the rosy-fingered dawn'.

According to legend, Helios would arise every morning and climb into his winged chariot, which was drawn by horses made of fire, and set off to ride across the sky. By midday he was directly overhead and then he began his descent, which was completed when he plunged into the ocean, where he would then rest on a golden bed fashioned for him by Hephaestos.

# Hermit

The first thing to mention about this word is that it is generally misspelled. The initial 'h' is historically incorrect and is due to the influence of Medieval Latin, which used the form *heremite*. The Late Latin form was *eremita* and the Old French had two spellings: one with the 'h' and one without: *ermit* and *hermit*. Medieval English almost certainly adopted the second alternative from the French.

Since 1799 we have tended to think of a hermit as somebody who prefers to shun society and live by himself. Strictly speaking, however, if we consider the literal meaning of the original Greek, a 'hermit' is somebody who lives in a desert. The Greek noun *erēmia* (ἐρημία) meant 'desert', 'wilderness', and by extension 'solitude', 'loneliness'.

In about the year 1200 the more scholarly form of the word, 'eremite', appeared in English, which was a closer reflection of the original Greek. It is still used in English but is usually confined to specialist contexts.


# Hero

Television and newspaper reports often refer to 'have-a-go heroes' who step in to prevent street crime. And almost anyone who displays courage 'above and beyond the call of duty', whether on the battlefield, the sports field or even the high street, is referred to nowadays as a 'hero'.

This generalized usage was first noted in the 1660s; as a designation of the main character in a play it dates from the 1690s.

The word entered English in the fourteenth century, meaning 'demigod', via French, from Ancient Greek, in which *herōs* (ἥρως) originally had a much more specific definition. Hesiod, the farmer poet, defined the heroes as a divine race of demigods (representing the fourth out of five 'ages of deterioration') who appeared on Earth during the latter part of the Bronze Age. Despite their superhuman strength and courage, they were destroyed in battles outside Thebes and Troy and their place was taken by the fifth 'age of deterioration', the Men of Iron.

Later in Greek history the term was applied to mythical beings, such as Herakles and Theseus, who had one human parent and one divine.

# Herpes

The painful inflammatory skin condition that spreads over the body at what can seem an alarming rate was first termed 'herpes' by English doctors in the late fourteenth century.

The word was taken from the Latin *herpes*, which had been adapted from the original Greek verb *herpein* (ἕρπειν), 'to creep', 'to crawl', applied normally to creatures that slide, creep or crawl over the ground. The associated noun *herponta* (ἕρποντα) was used to describe all creeping things, in much the same way as we refer to 'creepy-crawlies'.

The Greek *herpein* had its cognate equivalent in the Latin *serpere*, also 'to creep', with its derivative noun *serpo*, from which we derive our older term for a snake, 'serpent'. Therefore modern English 'herpes', the creeping rash, and 'serpent', the creature that creeps though the grass, are linguistically closely related.

# Hieroglyph

There is a very basic question (but one which is usually overlooked) connected with this word. Most people are well aware that hieroglyphs are associated with the carvings or drawings on Egyptian monuments and artefacts, yet the word itself is not Egyptian but Greek. Why?

The answer lies with the Greek biographer and essayist Plutarch (*c.* 46–*c.* 120 CE), who was the first to refer to the ancient carvings he came across in Egypt as *hierogluphika* (ἱερογλυφικά), literally 'the sacred carvings'. The practice has persisted right up to the present day.

Plutarch's term was derived from the Greek singular adjective *hierogluphikos* (ἱερογλυφικός), 'pertaining to the sacred carvings', comprising *hieros* (ἱερός), 'sacred', and *gluphein* (γλύφειν), 'to carve'.

'Hieroglyphics' has been applied to the Egyptian writing system since the 1580s in English.

## History

This academic study of the past involves a lot of rooting about in libraries, archives and other sources of information offering rich pickings for the avid 'historian'. And such activities offer an explanation of the origin of the word. The Greek noun *historia* (ἱστορία) could be defined as an account of things learned by asking questions and making detailed enquiries, so perhaps the best translation of the word would be 'research'. The root verb here is *historein* (ἱστορεῖν), 'to learn by enquiry', 'to question'.

As a methodological account of events the word has featured in English since the fifteenth century. Its application to the study of natural phenomena (as in 'natural history') dates from the sixteenth century.

## GREEK HISTORIANS

### Herodotos

Generally recognized as 'the father of history', not because he was the first person to produce accounts of historical events, but because he was the first to attempt analytical and critical evaluations of them.

He was born in Halicarnassus (modern Bodrum in Turkey) around the year 484 BCE. He lived for several years in Athens before setting off on a journey which would take him away from Greece. Some believe he travelled in Egypt, Asia and even around the part of the world we would now think of as Eastern Europe. He eventually settled down in Southern Italy in 433 BCE.

His major contribution to historical studies was the *Histories,* his nine-volume account of the war in which the Persians suffered major defeats in 490 and 480 BCE when they attempted to invade Greece.

### Thucydides

He was born in Halimous (modern Alimos) in Greece around 460 BCE. Frequently referred to as 'the father of scientific history' because of his insistence on detached impartiality in historical reporting, he tells us in *History of the Peloponnesian War* (fought between Athens and Sparta) that he contracted the plague and was one of the few who survived. This encouraged him to take an interest in how ordinary people react emotionally and psychologically to wars, massacres and natural disasters.

Thucydides fought as a general in the war (Sparta defeated Athens in 404 BCE) but appears not to have returned from the field of battle covered in glory. In fact, because of his poor showing he was banished for twenty years. He died suddenly, back in Athens, c.400 BCE.

## Xenophon

Historian, soldier and philosopher (he was a student of Socrates), Xenophon was born in Athens c.430 BCE. Possibly his main work was the *Hellenica*, which took up largely where Thucydides broke off, recounting the final seven years of the Peloponnesian War and its aftermath.

In 401 BCE he enrolled as a Greek mercenary and went off to war in support of the Persian prince, Cyrus. When Cyrus died Xenophon assumed command of the Greeks and famously led 10,000 men back home. The trek turned out to be a 1,000-mile slog through enemy territory. According to his account of the campaign in the *Anabasis*, when the soldiers caught their first glimpse of the Euxine or Black Sea they yelled out in unison *Thalassa! Thalassa!* (θάλασσα), 'The sea! The sea!' This became one of the most famous quotations in Greek history. He died in the Peloponnese in 354 BCE.

# Hoi polloi

There are not many Greek expressions, by comparison with Latin, that have been adopted into English in their complete original form, but *hoi polloi* (οἱ πολλοί) is one of them.

It is used now to refer, usually rather contemptuously, to the masses or what used to be termed the 'lower classes', but in fact it means nothing more than 'the many'. The expression only acquired its pejorative meaning in the nineteenth century; an equivalent, similarly dismissive, Greek term was *agoraioi* (ἀγοραῖοι), 'those who hang around the market'.

The term was first used in an English context by the poet Dryden in 1668, although he quoted it in Greek. Its first use in transliterated form is thought to date from 1837.

It is not uncommon to hear people talk about 'the hoi polloi', not realizing that they are repeating themselves: *hoi* meant 'the' in Ancient Greek (technically speaking, the masculine plural of the definite article), so introducing the expression with English 'the' is redundant repetition.

*Polloi* is the plural form of *polus* (πολύς), meaning 'much', which produced the prefix *poly-*, frequently used in English in combination with other words of Greek origin. These include:

| | |
|---|---|
| *polyandry* | having more than one husband |
| *polyanthus* | bearing many flowers |
| *polyclinic* | clinic treating more than one type of disease |
| *polygamy* | having more than one wife (strictly: more than one marriage) |
| *polyglot* | speaking more than one language |
| *polygon* | having many angles |
| *polymath* | learned in many subjects |
| *polynesia* | literally 'many islands' |
| *polyphagous* | eating many types of food |
| *polytheism* | belief in more than one god |

# Horizon

Before the Norman invasion in 1066, the Old English term *eaggemearc*, literally 'eye mark', was used to mean 'the furthest point the eye can see'. As Norman French began to supplant the native language, the term *orizon*, borrowed directly from the Latin *horizon*, had gradually replaced the Old English term by the fourteenth century.

But the Latin noun had been adopted from the earlier Greek expression *horizōn kuklos* (ὁρίζων κύκλος), which did not denote a straight line in the distance, as we understand the word, but 'the limiting circle'. This was a reference to the Greek understanding of the word *kuklos* in this context as 'the vault of Heaven', the adjective *horizōn* being, strictly speaking, the present participle of the verb *horizein* (ὁρίζειν), 'to limit', 'to define'. The related noun *horos* (ὅρος) meant 'a boundary' or 'limit'.

As late as the sixteenth century the associated adjective 'horizontal' was used to denote objects or places considered to be 'close to the horizon'; the meaning we attach to the word today, namely 'flat' or 'parallel to the horizon', did not appear in English until the 1630s.

The initial 'h' was restored to the English spelling, influenced by the Latin, in the seventeenth century.

# Hour

The word 'hour' has since the Middle Ages defined a specific period of time: sixty minutes. Prior to that the term was far less accurate or specific. As late as the thirteenth century, for example, it was still used in the Church to mean simply a period of time set aside for quiet contemplation and prayer.

It came into English from French, which had the word *ore* (alternatively spelled *hore*) as a canonical hour, and was adopted from the Latin *hora*, which could designate an hour but could also be applied in literature or poetry to any of the four seasons or a time of year.

The degree of imprecision associated with the early use of this word becomes clearer when we consider the original Greek from which the Latin, Old French and Middle English were taken. *Hōra* (ὥρα) could mean any time of day or night, as in *hōra nuktos* (ὥρα νυκτός, 'night time'); any season or, more generally, 'time' – as in modern English expressions such as 'a fitting time', 'the wrong time', 'the time of one's life'.

One close linguistic relative which crops up regularly in even the most serious of newspapers is 'horoscope'. The original Greek term was *hōroscopos* (ὡροσκόπος), from the verb *hōroskopein* (ὡροσκοπειν), 'to observe the hour [of birth]'.

Perhaps confusingly, the same Indo-European word that produced 'hour' is closely connected to that which gave us the word 'year'.

## Hubris

The violent associations understood by the original Greek word are usually forgotten when this word is used in a modern context. Most people use it to mean 'excessive pride', frequently of the kind that goes before a fall. The original Greek *hubris* (ὕβρις), however, meant 'wanton destructiveness', 'violent aggression', and was considered an offence against the gods. The connection with pride is explained by the Greeks' recognition that those who commit such outrages are frequently spurred on by feelings of power and superiority generated by harming and/ or humiliating others.

The word entered English in the nineteenth century when it was interpreted as 'wanton insolence'.

## Hulk

The word was first applied in English in the sixteenth century to lumbering, clumsy people of ungainly build. By the seventeenth century the description was being additionally applied to the cumbersome merchant ships that had outlived their usefulness and were now lying beached on some seashore or river bank, unloved, unwanted and left to rot.

In Old English a *hulk* was a light ship, but by the Middle Ages the word *hulke* was virtually synonymous with any ship. And both terms were related to the Medieval Latin *holcas*, a direct borrowing from the Greek *holkas* (ὁλκάς), a large merchant ship that had to be towed onto the beach by means of a *holkos* (ὁλκός), a kind of winch designed specifically for the purpose. Both nouns are derived from the verb *helkein* (ἕλκειν), 'to haul', 'to drag'. There is a fascinating etymological link here. When *holkos* (ὁλκός) was used as an adjective it meant 'attractive', a modern English word derived from the Latin *ad*, 'towards', and *trahere*, 'to drag', 'to pull', so that if we find someone 'attractive' we are admitting that we are 'drawn towards' them.

---

## WATER, WATER EVERYWHERE...

One of the very first Greek philosophers was Thales of Miletus (*c.*624–546 BCE). With the benefit of historical hindsight we can safely say that he was a remarkable thinker, way ahead of his time. He is credited with predicting the solar eclipse of 585 BCE, making contributions to mathematics and geometry, and being the first person to attempt to understand the world and the universe by reason and logic rather than a reliance on mythological explanations.

He is best known, however, for his observations of matter. He studied the physical world about him and came to the conclusion that the prime material, present in all matter, was water.

# Hydraulic

As an adjective meaning simply 'relating to how fluids behave when in motion', the word 'hydraulic' has been used in English since about 1600. By the 1670s it had acquired a more specific application as a plural noun 'hydraulics' defining the scientific study of what happens when fluids (strictly speaking, 'water') move of their own volition or are made to move by technical means.

The derivation of the word is the Greek *hudraulikos* or *hydraulikos* (ὑδραυλικός), 'relating to a *hudraulis* or *hydraulis* (ὕδραυλις), an early type of musical instrument operated by water being pumped through reeds or pipes. And this word is a combination of the Greek for water, *hudōr* or *hydōr* (ὕδωρ), and *aulos* (αὐλός), 'reed', 'tube'.

The prefix 'hydro-' is now a common prefix in English and always indicates a relationship with water. But there are also some words in English formed directly from the Greek root and, again, they always suggest a close affinity with water: 'dehydrated' (lacking water); 'hydrogen' (a gas forming water when in contact with oxygen); 'hydrangea' (a flower which retains water in its seed pods); 'hydrophobia' (rabies, a disease characterized by a fear of water). It is also a distant relative of the word 'otter', related to *hudros* or *hydros* (ὕδρος), a 'water snake'.

## Hygiene

In the seventeenth century English borrowed the word *hygiene* from French; in both languages, however, the word's association was more with health than with cleanliness, as the Greek derivative noun was *hugieia* (ὑγίεια), meaning 'health', 'soundness of body'. The modern English meaning of cleanliness dates only from the nineteenth century.

### HUGIEIA

The Greeks' predilection for personifying everything connected with the human condition found a perfect subject in the health and well-being of mortal men and women.

Hygiene (or Hugieia) was portrayed in Greek mythology as the goddess of health and sanitation. She was the daughter of Asclepios, the god of medicine, and Epionē, the goddess of the soothing of pain. Her four sisters (and inseparable companions) were:

| | |
|---|---|
| *Panacea* | the goddess of universal remedy |
| *Iasō* | the goddess of recuperation |
| *Akesō* | the goddess of the healing process |
| *Aglaia* | the goddess of beauty, splendour and adornment |

# Hypnotism

In Britain in the 1620s the word 'hypnotic' was being used by the medical profession to describe drugs which were known to induce sleep or drowsiness. In the nineteenth century a certain Dr James Braid of Manchester coined the expression 'neuro-hypnotism', literally the practice of 'putting the nerves to sleep', but this was soon shortened to simply 'hypnotism'. This was the age when scientists were becoming increasingly fascinated by the discoveries of Friedrich Anton Mesmer (1734–1815) – his theories of animal magnetism and the strange fluids that coursed through our veins and allowed some people to induce a trance-like sleep in others. And of course Dr Mesmer gave rise to the alternative term to hypnotism, 'mesmerism'.

'Hypnotism', 'hypnotize', 'hypnosis' and 'hypnotic' are all derived from the Greek word for sleep *hupnos* or *hypnos* (ὕπνος) and the verb *hupnoun* or *hypnoun* (ὑπνοῦν), 'to lull to sleep'.

In Greek mythology sleep was personified as Hupnos or Hypnos (Ὕπνος), the twin brother of Thanatos (Θάνατος), Death, and not even the gods were able to escape their power and influence.


# Hypochondria

The dictionary tells us that a 'hypochondriac' suffers from a morbid, unfounded conviction that he or she is suffering from any number of medical complaints. When the word was first used in English in the early seventeenth century it simply described a sad individual who was prone to despair; the modern meaning dates from the eighteenth century.

The origin of the word is the Greek *hupochondria* (ὑποχόνδρια), formed from *hupo* or *hypo* (ὑπό), 'under', and *chondros* (χόνδρος), 'gristle', 'cartilage'. The significance of the cartilage is that in the early days of medicine it was commonly believed that feelings of sadness and depression emanated from a site just under the cartilage behind the breastbone.

## Hypocrisy

The twelfth-century version of this word in English was *ipocrisie*, from the French *ypocrisie* and the Late Latin *hypocrisis*, which had a precise meaning: 'imitation of the gestures and speech of another'. At the root of the Late Latin expression, however, lies the Greek *hupokrisis* (ὑπόκρισις), originally 'acting on stage' but later used to define any act of 'pretending' or 'playing a part', whether literally or metaphorically.

In the world of Greek theatre, the *hupocritēs* or *hypocritēs* (ὑποκριτής) was the term for 'an actor', but with the passage of time the word acquired the additional meaning of 'dissembler'. The meaning we attach to the word today dates from the thirteenth century.

# Hysteria

In the very early nineteenth century, when members of the medical profession were looking for a term to define a certain nervous condition characterized by an extreme lack of self-control, they decided on 'hysteria'. As the condition seemed to affect women far more than men, they assumed that it must stem from the uniquely feminine part of the human body, the womb. They therefore adopted the Greek term *hustera* or *hystera* (ὑστέρα), 'womb', 'belly', a close relative of another common medical term, uterus.

Ultimately the Greek *hustera* or *hystera* (ὑστέρα) is linguistically related to *outhar* (οὖθαρ), 'breast', and another term for a milk-producing gland, 'udder'.

# Idea

The basic concept behind this word, which is first attested in English in the sixteenth century, is that when we think of something we 'see' it in our mind's eye. The Greek noun, from which our word is derived, was *idea* (ἰδέα), from the verb *idein* (ἰδεῖν), 'to see'.

For the Greeks, however, the word had a slightly more precise meaning: they applied it to the appearance of an object or person as distinct from their true nature.

## Idiosyncrasy

Our idiosyncrasies are the fads, foibles and individual character traits that go towards making up our character. The word has been used in English since the seventeenth century. It was borrowed from the French, who borrowed it from the Greek *idiosugkrasia* (ἰδιοσυγκρασία), 'personal temperament', which comprises three elements: *idios* (ἴδιος), 'one's own'; *sun* (σύν), 'together with'; and *krasis* (κρᾶσις), 'mixture'. The implication here is that originally a person's 'idiosyncrasy' comprised those personality traits that combined in such a way as to make him or her unique.

There is an interesting comparison to be made here with Latin. The Latin verb *temperare* meant 'to mix', and its associated noun *temperamentum*, 'mixture', is the origin of the modern English 'temperament'.

## Idiot

We tend to bandy this word around in everyday speech, applying it to just about anybody we think of as not being among the most intelligent. This is a bit odd, as the original Greek word was simply applied to people who displayed little interest in politics. The Greek *idiotēs* (ἰδιότης) meant 'private citizen' or 'layman', and described individuals who kept themselves to themselves and pre-ferred not to take part in the affairs of state or even local government. To the Greeks such people appeared very unusual or strange. By the time the word reached English in the thirteenth century it had acquired the additional associations with ignorance and less than adequate intellectual ability.

## Idyllic

This adjective has been used in English since the 1830s to describe almost any scene full of rustic charm evoking a sanitized version of life in the countryside.

It is derived from the Latin *idyllium* and the Greek *eidullion* (εἰδύλλιον), both of which were terms for short, highly descriptive poems, usually dealing with rural themes and country folk. The Greek term was related to the noun *eidos* (εἶδος), meaning literally 'that which has been seen' but usually translated as 'form' or 'shape' or 'little picture'.

The use of the derivative noun 'idyll' to define a short descriptive pastoral poem dates from the seventeenth century.

## Imp

Since the 1640s we have been referring to naughty little children as 'imps', a title which, deservedly or not, hearkens back to an expression which was used in the sixteenth century, 'imp of Satan'. But an 'imp' of Satan would not have been one of his little devils as the word at that time meant nothing more than 'offspring', 'child'.

This meaning was attached to the word from the late fourteenth century; prior to that its use was restricted to the world of botany and agriculture. It came into Old English (which had *impe* or *impa* for 'young shoot' or 'graft') from the Late Latin *impotus*, which meant 'implanted', a direct borrowing of the Greek *emphutos* (ἔμφυτος), 'inborn' or 'innate'. This adjective was derived from the compound verb *emphuein* (ἐμφύειν), 'to implant', comprising *em* for *en* (ἐν), 'in', and *phuein* (φύειν), 'to beget', 'to generate'.


## Ink

There can be few words that look more English than this, but it is in fact of Greek origin. The Late Roman emperors used a substance known as *encaustum* for signing important documents, having borrowed it from the Greeks, who referred to it as *enkauston* (ἔγκαυστον), 'that which has been burned into'. This was a word made up from *en* (ἐν), 'in', and *kaiein* (καίειν), 'to burn', as the substance's original use was to 'burn' designs into tiles. Another closely related word in English is 'caustic'.

'Ink' entered English in the thirteenth century, originally being spelled in Middle English as *enke*, which perhaps mirrors the derivation of the word more than the modern spelling does.

# Kaleidoscope

In 1817 the Scottish inventor Sir David Brewster (1781–1868) needed a name for his newly invented optical toy, which amazed its users with its infinite display of beautiful, highly coloured shapes. Basically, the toy consisted of a tube in two sections; when the observer looked through it, turning one of the sections as he or she did so, a myriad of shapes and colours became visible on a screen at the far end. The toy sold in its thousands and, although the inventor's lack of business acumen meant that he never made any money from it, it was a source of joy and wonderment to generations of children (and not a few adults).

The name Brewster hit on for his invention was 'kaleidoscope', made up of three Greek words: *kalos* (καλός), 'beautiful'; *eidos* (εἶδος), 'shape'; and *skopein* (σκοπεῖν), 'to see'. So the toy was simply a tube that allowed a user to 'see beautiful shapes'.

Although, in an age when children prefer more sophisticated playthings, the kaleidoscope has ceased to be as popular as it once was, the word is still used figuratively as a description of rapidly changing scenes or colours.

# Know

The verb 'to know' cannot claim to be descended from a Greek word but it is a very close relative of the verb *gignōskein* (γιγνώσκειν), 'to know'. Both words (along with the Latin *gnoscere*) are derived from the postulated Indo-European root *\*gno* and are therefore more accurately described as being 'cognate'.

When the word first appeared in English in the eleventh century it was closer in meaning to 'recognize'. Its use to mean 'being familiar with certain facts or information' was a later, twelfth-century, development.

Since the thirteenth century the derivative adjective 'noble' has applied to the 'nobility'; that is, those at the top of the social pile, who are more likely to be 'known' or 'recognized' by the general populace than those further down the social scale.

*gnōthi seauton*

γνῶθι σεαυτόν

'know thyself'

GREEK PROVERB

# Kudos

This word was first noted in English around the year 1800 and is thought to have been introduced to the language by university students, no doubt attempting to display their erudition and knowledge of the classics. Perhaps they believed that by demonstrating their familiarity with such an arcane subject as Greek they would acquire a certain amount of 'kudos' and a reputation for scholarship.

The word itself has a noble and ancient heritage; it was used by Homer to mean 'glory' or 'fame', particularly of the sort acquired through prowess on the battlefield. In the *Iliad* we read of the *mega kudos tōn akhaiōn* (μέγα κῦδος τῶν Ἀχαιῶν), 'the great glory of the Achaeans' (i.e. the Greeks).

## Laconic

Anybody described as being 'laconic' will be extremely economical with his or her words; answers to questions will be brief, to the point and with no unnecessary embellishment or superfluous verbiage. The original Greek word was *lakōnikos* (λακωνικός), the primary meaning of which was 'relating to the area of Lakonia'. Lakonia was, and is, the area surrounding Sparta; 'laconic', then, is an alternative word for 'Spartan'.

Its application in English to those of few words dates from the late sixteenth century, but the original 'laconic' reply dates from Philip of Macedon's threat to the Spartans. He told them that if he attacked Sparta he would raze it to the ground. The 'laconic' reply was 'If'.

## Lamp

In ancient Rome people used candles to find their way around at night, but in Ancient Greece candles were unknown. The most usual form of illumination there was the torch; then came little dishes with oil and a wick, which burned slowly and with just enough 'candle power' to allow people to find their way around the house or to venture abroad. Once lit, the oil lamps 'shone'; the Greek for 'to shine' was *lampein* (λάμπειν). The little container for the burning oil was known as a *lampas* (λαμπάς), the origin of our word 'lamp'. Interestingly, the Ancient Greeks did not use  the verb solely in a visual context. A light could 'shine', but a clear, distinct sound was also described as *lampros* (λαμπρός), 'bright'.

'Lamp' first entered English *c.*1200 as a borrowing of the French *lampe*, the normal word for the device in twelfth-century France. This had been acquired from the Latin *lampas*, obviously taken from the Greek without any attempt to alter the word at all.

But, of course, in ancient times there were other sources of light in addition to oil. Wood, coal and charcoal all provided ample sources of heat, and no doubt light, when the fire was big enough and the glow inviting. The Greeks even had what is best described as their equivalent of a modern electric standard lamp; it consisted of a column of bronze topped with a bowl holding burning charcoal or blazing splinters of pinewood. Such a source of light was known as a *lamptēr* (λαμπτήρ).

The Greek for charcoal and live coals was *anthrax* (ἄνθραξ), a term adopted into English for the first time in 1398 to identify the disease characterized by the black and red lesions, resembling burning coals, on the skins of animals (and occasionally humans) infected with the bacterium *Bacillus anthracis*.

## Lethargy

We have used this word in English to describe enervating feelings of torpor and a lack of energy since the fourteenth century; it is a direct borrowing from the Greek *lēthargia* (ληθαργία), 'drowsiness'. But the Greek noun is itself a combination of *lēthē* (λήθη), 'forgetfulness', and *argos* (ἀργός), 'laziness', 'lack of energy'. So we could say that a person described as 'lethargic' is, strictly speaking, someone who forgets what he or she is supposed to be doing and is too bone idle to do it anyway!

## Liquorice

In ancient times the sweet root which is now known in English as liquorice was thought of as having considerable health benefits. In the Middle Ages it was spelled *licoriz*, an adapted form of the Late Latin *liquirita*. This in turn was a contracted spelling of the Greek *glukurriza* (γλυκύρριζα), comprising the Greek words *glukus* (γλυκύς), 'sweet', and (*rhiza*) (ῥίζα), 'root'. Another related word is

According to Greek mythology there were five rivers surrounding the underworld, the destination of the souls of the recent dead. One of these rivers was *Lēthē*, the river of oblivion or forgetfulness. The Greeks believed that all souls, having begun their journey to the afterlife, had to drink from this river in order to forget their past lives and to prepare for what was to come, unencumbered by regrets or memories and a longing to return to their former state. The associated verb here is *lanthanesthai*, 'to forget'. The other four rivers of the underworld were: *Acherōn*, the river of sorrow; *Styx*, the river of hatred; *Kokytos*, the river of lamentation; *Phlegethōn*, the river of fire.

'glucose', also derived from *glukus* via the derivative noun *gleukos* (γλεῦκος), 'sweet wine'.

# Machine

Words such as 'machine', 'mechanic', 'mechanism' and so on all derive from the same Greek root, *mēchos* (μῆχος), a 'means' or 'contrivance'. It also produced another closely related word, *mēchanē* (μηχανή), defining any contrivance, instrument or device specifically designed for lifting heavy weights. This was also the term used for an 'engine of war'. In the sixteenth century it was used as a generic term for almost any kind of structure. Since the seventeenth it has been applied to any apparatus designed to apply mechanical power.

> *tas mēchanas meta ton polemon komizeis*
>
> τάς μηχανὰς μετὰ τὸν πόλεμον κομίζεις
>
> 'you are delivering the engine of war after the war'
>
> GREEK PROVERB

## Magic

The magicians who entertain us on stage, screen and children's parties can trace the origins of their art back to the countries of the Middle East before the birth of Christ. In fact, the Magi (also known as the Three Wise Men in the Nativity story) were 'magicians' who claimed to be able to interpret dreams, foretell the future and demonstrate other supernatural skills.

The Greek word for the noun 'magic' (borrowed from the Old Persian word, *magus*, 'wise man' and member of the Persian priestly class) was *mageia* (μᾰγεία), an abbreviated form of *mageutikē technē* (μαγευτική τέχνη), 'magic art' or 'the art of the Magi'.

The word was first used in English in the fourteenth century, borrowed from the Old French *magique*, which in turn had been acquired from the Late Latin *magica*, taken from the Greek.

# Magnet

As a term for oxide of iron, the word 'magnet' was known in English in the fifteenth century (its associated element 'magnesia' was an essential ingredient in the world of alchemy). By the seventeenth century the term was being applied to any piece of iron or steel which demonstrated properties of attraction.

'Magnet' entered English in the mid-1400s from the Old French *magnete*, derived from the Latin *magnes*, a direct borrowing from the Greek, which had either *magnēs lithos* (μάγνης λίθος) or *magnētis lithos* (μαγνῆτις λίθος), literally 'the stone from Magnesia'. Magnesia could either refer to the Lydian city Magnesia (modern-day Manisa in Turkey) or an area of Thessaly in central Greece. The latter was a region renowned throughout the ancient world as the source of rocks which, when suspended on a piece of thread, always pointed north–south and so provided the first primitive compasses.

The alternative term for a 'magnet', of course, is 'lodestone', now used figuratively or for historical interest. This comprises two words, *lode* (the Old English for 'way') and 'stone', as it was a piece of rock useful to travellers who needed to know which 'way' to go.


# Maniac

When this word entered English in the fourteenth century it denoted anyone driven by a highly excited form of madness; it retains much of this meaning today. The original Greek word was *mania* (μανία), 'madness', a derivative of the verb *mainesthai* (μαίνεσθαι), 'to be driven mad', 'to be driven into a rage'.

Over the years psychologists have invented and devised hundreds of 'manias' simply by combining Greek words with the suffix '-mania'. Here are a few of them:

| | |
|---|---|
| *kleptomania* | obsession with stealing |
| *dipsomania* | obsession with drinking |
| *ergomania* | compulsion to work |
| *dromomania* | compulsion to travel |
| *megalomania* | delusions of grandeur |
| *mythomania* | compulsion to lie or exaggerate |
| *xenomania* | exaggerated interest in foreign customs |
| *thanatomania* | exaggerated fascination with death |
| *orchestromania* | obsession with dancing |
| *phagomania* | obsessive need to eat |

## Margarine

Napoleon III of France (1808–1873) was so concerned about feeding his soldiers and helping the poor that he offered a prize to anyone who could invent a substitute for butter, a rather expensive food item at the time. A certain Hippolyte Mège-Mouriès, continuing the work done by an earlier French chemist, won the prize, but of course had to find a name for his new product. His predecessor, Eugène Chevreul, had in 1813 come up with the term *oleomargarine* because it comprised natural oil (*oleo*) and had a certain sheen to it which reminded him of the surface of a pearl, the Greek for which is *margarités* (μαργαρίτης). Hippolyte simply discarded the first element of the word and retained the second.

## Marmalade

Anyone who has had a look at other languages will probably be aware that some form of this word exists in most European languages and refers to what we would think of as 'jam' or, in the case of France, stewed fruit. Since the seventeenth century, however, English has applied the word 'marmalade' specifically to jam made from citrus fruits, such as oranges and lemons.

The word entered English in the late fifteenth or early sixteenth century from French, which had acquired it from the Portuguese term *marmalada*, derived from the word for the fruit we know as 'quince', *marmelo*. The Portuguese word evolved from the Latin *melimelum*, originally the term for the fruit of an apple tree which had been grafted onto a quince tree. Tracing the origin of this word even further back, we find that it comprised two earlier Greek words, *meli* (μέλι), 'honey', and *mēlon* (μῆλον), 'apple'. And, yes, the same Greek word gave us our 'melon'.

The Greek for 'quince' was *mēlon kudōnion* (μῆλον κυδώνιον), literally an apple from Kudōn, a city in Crete.

Closely related to the Greek word for honey was the word *melissa* (μέλισσα) or *melitta* (μέλιττα), a 'bee'.

## Mathematics

The basic Greek verb from which this word is derived was *manthanein* (μανθάνειν), 'to learn'. The derivative noun *mathēmata* (μαθήματα) simply meant 'those things that have been learned'; another related plural noun, *mathēmatika* (μαθηματικά), was applied specifically to the branch of learning associated with figures and calculations – or, as we would say, 'mathematics'. This probably explains why the English 'mathematics' is always spoken of as being plural.

The word 'mathematics' was adopted into English in the sixteenth century; it is a distant linguistic relative of the word 'mind'. The first syllable of *manthanein* is related to the Indo-European root *men*, which has provided words such as the Latin *mens* (mind, intellect) and hence the English 'mind', 'mental' and so on.

> *pathei mathos*
>
> πάθει μάθος
>
> 'suffer and learn'
>
> AESCHYLUS, *AGAMEMNON*

## Measure

This word can be used in several ways. We can 'measure' the size of something; we can know 'the measure' of someone; and we can behave in a calm and 'measured way'. All of these uses can trace their derivations back to the basic concepts behind the original Greek.

As an alternative to the word 'size' (as in 'the measurements of') the word has been used in English since the late fourteenth century. Around the year 1300 it was an instrument for taking the measurements of something, but later on, in the 1590s, it was a term for the specific treatment that could be meted out to those thought deserving of punishment or reward. And this meaning is reflected in the title of Shakespeare's play *Measure for Measure*, written in 1603 or 1604, the principal theme of which is the delicate balance between justice and mercy.

The Old English word for 'measure' was *meath* (*mæð*), derived from the Latin noun *mensura*, and the verb *metiri*, 'to measure', 'to estimate', 'to assess', particularly in the business of trading in grain. This is cognate with the Greek *metron* (μέτρον), 'a measure', 'a rule' or 'a standard', which of course is also the derivation of words such as 'metre', 'meter' and 'metric'. The derivative verb was *metrein* (μετρεῖν), 'to measure', 'to count', 'to estimate'.

> *ho anthrōpos pantōn metron*
>
> ὁ ἄνθρωπος πάντων μέτρον
>
> 'man is the measure of all things'
>
> PROTAGORAS

## Melody

Now used almost exclusively in English as a synonym for 'tune', the Old French term *melodie*, which we borrowed in the thirteenth century, meant all of 'music', 'tune' and 'song'. And the Greek words, from which both the French and English terms were derived, *melos* (μέλος), 'a song', and *melōdia* (μελῳδία), 'singing', originated in the verb *melpein* (μέλπειν), 'to sing'.

Closely connected, of course, is the noun 'melodrama', a term coined in the eighteenth century from the original Greek. It was applied to stage productions which were basically dramas with happy endings, accompanied by appropriate music reflecting the changing emotional states of the actors performing on stage.

## Metabolism

This has been the technical term since 1878 for the chemical changes that occur in an organism under certain circumstances. It is frequently used by dieticians, who encourage us to lose weight by 'speeding up the metabolism', by which they mean the body's efficiency in converting food into energy.

The derivation of the word is the Greek *metabolē* (μεταβολή), which simply means 'change'. The noun comprises two parts: the prefix *meta* (μετά), implying change, and the verb *ballein* (βάλλειν), 'to throw'. When these are brought together they form another verb, *metaballein* (μεταβάλλειν), meaning literally 'to throw in a different direction', or, figuratively, 'to alter the course of'.

> metabolē pantōn gluku
>
> μεταβολὴ πάντων γλυκύ
>
> 'a change in everything is sweet'
>
> GREEK PROVERB

## Meteorology

This word is now used exclusively with reference to the study of the weather and the ability to forecast its behaviour. It was first used in English in about 1610 and was a borrowing from the French *météorologie*. A few years later, in the 1620s, the term 'meteorologist' appeared to describe someone who was making tentative steps at being able to predict the weather. In the sixteenth century, such a person had been referred to as a 'meteorologician'.

The original Greek expression, however, reflects the Greek thinkers' preoccupation with the heavens and the contents therein: the stars, Sun, Moon, clouds, and so on.

The basic verb at the centre is *hairein* (αἴρειν), 'to lift', and the emphatic prefix μετα- (μετα-), combining to produce both *metairein* (μεταίρειν), 'to lift up high', and another verb with the same meaning, *meteōrizein* (μετεωρίζειν). This is a derivative of the plural noun *meteōra* (μετέωρα), 'things lifted up high'.

## ASTRONOMER OR ASTROLOGER?

Strictly speaking an 'astronomer' studies the 'laws of
the stars' and how they are 'distributed' throughout
the heavens. The word is derived from *astēr*, 'star', and
*nomos*, 'law' or 'distribution'. 'Astronomy', as the word is
used today, has nothing to do with studying the heavenly bodies in an attempt to predict the future.
'Astrologers', on the other hand, believe that by making
complicated charts showing the position of various stars
and planets at the moment of birth it is possible to predict
what effect it will have on a person's life. Few genuine
scientists today believe this to be anything other than a
bit of fun and that such predictions should not be taken
seriously. In Ancient Greece, however, the astrologers were
taken very seriously and their art ranked highly among
other techniques at learned men's disposal when clients
(statesmen, generals, politicians and ordinary members of
the public) needed to know what the future held in store
for them.

Linguistically, matters were rather complicated for
the Greeks. Their word for an 'astronomer' was *astrono-
mos*; but there was in addition the term *astrologos*, which
also meant 'astronomer'. Eventually the two definitions
diverged and the *astrologos* came to be associated with
what we now think of as an 'astrologer'.

But the complications continue. Another Greek
term for an 'astronomer' was *meteōrologos*, our 'meteorologist', and an alternative term for an 'astrologer' was
*meteōrosophistēs*, literally 'a man who is 'wise', 'learned'
(*sophos*) in matters concerning 'the things on high'.

Combined with *logos* (λόγος), 'the study of', it produced *meteorologia* (μετεορολογία), 'a treatise concerning heavenly bodies', the original meaning of the word we use in English today.

And, of course, the phenomenon we refer to as a 'meteor' is exactly the same word and originally meant simply 'something lifted up high'.


## *Migraine*

The particular type of headache which affects only half of the brain has been known in English since the fourteenth century when the condition was spelled 'megrin'. This was altered in the eighteenth century to 'migraine' and was itself a contraction of the Latin *hemicrania*. The Greeks, who originally came up with a term for the 'half-brain' headache, called it the *hēmikrania* (ἡμικρανία), which literally means 'half the head', derived from the prefix *hēmi-* (ἡμι-), 'half', and *kranion* (κράνιον), 'the upper part of the head'.

> *archē hēmisu pantōn*
>
> ἀρχὴ ἥμισυ πάντων
>
> 'the beginning is half of everything'
>
> GREEK PROVERB

## Monarchy

The 'constitutional monarchy' under which the people of the United Kingdom live disguises somewhat the derivation of the word 'monarchy'. The Queen now is more of a symbolic rather than an actual ruler as her powers are strictly limited by Parliament. The original 'monarchs', however, were absolute rulers whose word was law, and woe betide anyone who forgot it.

The word entered English in the mid-fourteenth century as a borrowing of the French *monarchie*, which in turn could trace its origins back to the Greek *monarchia* (μοναρχία). And this comprised *monos* (μόνος), 'single', 'alone', and the verb *archein* (ἄρχειν), 'to rule'. That is to say, 'monarchy' defined the system of government according to which the head of state 'ruled alone'.

## Monopoly

'Monopoly' first appeared in English at some point in the sixteenth century. It was adopted, perhaps by the politicians and businessmen of the day, from the Latin *monopolium*, to describe the legal right of a trader to deal exclusively in one commodity. This is a clue to the Greek origin of the word: *monopōlion* (μονοπώλιον) was a noun derived from a contraction of *monos* (μόνος), 'sole', and *pōlein* (πωλέιν), 'to sell'.

The verb 'to monopolize', meaning 'to dominate' or 'to take full control of' in a figurative, non-commercial sense, dates from the 1620s. The popular board game 'Monopoly' was patented in 1933 and first went on sale on 6 February 1935.

## Morphine

The opiate morphine, a powerful soporific, was originally termed 'morphium' by the early-nineteenth-century German chemist Friedrick Sertürner. He took the name from the Greek *Morpheus* (Μορφεύς), the god of dreams and son of Hupnos or Hypnos (Ύπνος), 'sleep'. The name Morpheus itself was derived from the noun *morphē* (μορφή), 'shape', 'form', and the verb *morphoun* (μορφοῦν), 'to mould', 'to shape', as in the world of Greek mythology he gave shape to the images people saw as they slept.

## Mouse

Not so very long ago a mouse was a pesky little rodent that appeared as an uninvited guest in many of our houses or featured as a cute little beastie in nursery rhymes and children's stories. Now most of us only come into contact with a 'mouse' when sitting at a desk and operating a computer.

It is a word which has been around for millennia and appears, with only slight modifications, in many Indo-European languages. Latin and Greek had *mus* (the latter written as μῦς), although for the Greeks the word had a double meaning. They had also spotted that the tiny rodent bore a remarkable resemblance to the anatomical feature we now refer to as a 'muscle' as it expanded and contracted beneath a person's skin.

The form 'muscle' appeared in English in the late fourteenth century, acquired from the Latin *musculus*, 'little mouse'. Later on the medical world adopted the root in the form of *myo-*, still used as a prefix for words associated with the musculature of the human frame.

The homophone 'mussel' also takes its spelling from the Latin and Greek roots, as the tiny sea creature reminded people in ancient times of the humble mouse. The change of spelling is first recorded in 1600 (perhaps as an attempt to distinguish between the seafood and the fibrous tissue) but it was not widely adopted until the second half of the nineteenth century.

## Moustache

The hair on the upper lip was first referred to in English as a 'moustache' in the sixteenth century. It was a borrowing of the Italian *mostaccio*, a word related directly to the Greek *moustakion* (μουστάκιον), the diminutive form of *mastaks* (μάσταξ), meaning generally 'the mouth' (literally 'the thing to chew with') but also more specifically 'the upper lip'. The same Greek noun was related to the verb *mastazein* (μαστάζειν), 'to chew', the derivation of the less common English synonym 'to masticate'.

Another derivative noun is *mastichē* (μαστίχη), the resin of the *schinos* (σχῖνος) tree, so-called because it was used in the East in ancient times in much the same way as chewing gum is used in the modern world. And *mastichē* is also the origin of our word 'mastic'. The *schinos* tree grows in particular abundance on the Greek island of Chios, where its resin is referred to as 'Chios tears'.

## Music

Surprisingly, the word 'music' does not appear in English before the mid-thirteenth century (the Old English *drēam* was used for 'music', 'joy', 'bliss', and is the source of the modern English 'dream'); it was introduced to the language from Norman French, which had *musique*, derived from the Latin word *musica*. The Latin word *musica* meant 'the art of music and poetry', no doubt a

## THE MUSES

In Greek mythology there were nine muses (all daughters of Zeus and Mnemosyne), each thought to be responsible for inspiring exponents of a given skill during moments of heightened creativity:

| | |
|---:|---|
| *Calliope* | epic poetry |
| *Clio* | history |
| *Erato* | love poetry, lyric art |
| *Euterpe* | music, particularly of the flute |
| *Melpomene* | tragedy |
| *Polymnia* | hymns |
| *Terpsichore* | dance |
| *Thalia* | comedy |
| *Urania* | astronomy |

The place where all the muses were thought to reside was termed a *mouseion* (μουσεῖον), 'Temple of the Muses', from which we derive the word 'museum'.

╼╾╼╾╼╾╼╾╼╾╼╾╼╾╼╾╼

reflection of the original Greek *mousikē technē* (μουσικὴ τέχνη), 'art of the muses', a generic term covering music, song, dance, poetry and what we would now refer to as the fine arts. The basis of the Greek phrase was *Mousai* (Μοῦσαι), the goddesses of the creative arts.

It appears that the Greeks first applied the word to poetry sung to a musical accompaniment; with the passage of time the poetry was forgotten and the word applied to the harmonic sounds alone.

# Myopic

If an optician tells us that we are 'myopic' he or she is informing us that we are short-sighted and probably need to correct the condition with suitable spectacles. Or we can use the adjective figuratively if we think someone's opinions have not been thought through properly and do not take into account their long-term consequences. But neither of these usages reflects the derivation of the word.

The first element, 'my', is from the Greek *muein* (μύειν), 'to close', and the second, *ops* (ὄψ), means 'eye'. So, technically speaking, the combination means 'to have one's eyes closed', but in fact the verb *muein* alone could have this meaning in Ancient Greek.

The meanings we attach to the adjective today date only from the seventeenth century.

# Myriad

This word has existed as a noun in English (a myriad of reasons...) since the 1550s and as an adjective (myriad reasons...) since the very early nineteenth century. Whether a noun or an adjective, the meaning is the same: a great number of something.

The origin of the word is the Greek adjective *murios* (μυρίος), which could mean either 'countless' when applied to numbers or 'immense', 'vast', 'infinite' in all other contexts. It even had a figurative usage as in the phrase *achos murion* (ἄχος μυρίον), 'endless grief'.

In the plural, *murioi* (μύριοι), the word could mean simply 'a vast number of', but it was also used with the specific meaning of 10,000. It is believed to be the largest number in Ancient Greek expressed by a single word.

## Mystery

Virtually anything we do not understand can now be described as 'a mystery'. It is a noun which entered English in the fourteenth century with the theological meaning of 'a religious truth or doctrine'. Towards the end of the fourteenth century its usage spread into the secular community where it was applied to anything the ordinary man (or woman) in the street found incomprehensible.

The word's immediate antecedents were the Old French *mistère*, 'a hidden meaning', and the earlier Latin plural noun *mysteria*, 'secret rites of divine worship'. Ultimately, both these terms can be traced back to the Greek *mustēria* (μυστήρια), which were secret ceremonies to which only a select group of initiates were admitted. They were people who had vowed not to talk about what went on at these ceremonies; they had promised, specifically, 'to keep their mouths shut', for which the Greek verb was *muein* (μύειν). So, we can safely assume, the original meaning of a 'mystery' was something about which the uninitiated knew nothing because those 'in the know' refused to talk about what they had seen at these secret rites. And the same verb *muein* is probably

## WHY THE CORN GROWS

The Eleusinian Mysteries were held every year in Eleusis, a suburb of Athens, in honour of Dēmēter ('Mother Earth') and her daughter Persephonē. This was the most famous and most important of the secret religious ceremonies in Ancient Greece and is thought to date back to an agrarian cult of the Mycenean era (c.1580–1100 BCE).

For those who had been initiated into the secret rites, the story of Persephonē symbolized the eternal nature of life as it was renewed by every generation. They also believed that possession of such knowledge would lead to their being handsomely rewarded in the afterlife.

According to the myth Dēmēter, the goddess of agriculture, had a daughter called Persephonē, who was abducted by Pluto and taken down to the underworld where she was to be his consort. Dēmēter attempted to get her daughter back but was only partially successful. As Persephonē had eaten pomegranate seeds in the underworld, thereby capturing the essence of life germinating below ground before bursting into bloom on its surface, she was not permitted to leave Hades entirely and was obliged to spend six months every year underground. When she was 'down below' no crops grew on the surface, but each spring and summer, when she had returned to her mother, the fields were full of golden corn.

This is how the Ancient Greeks explained the miracle of the Earth's beneficence once the dark days of winter were over for another year.

a distant etymological relative of the English adjective 'mute'. The first use of the word in English as a synonym for a detective novel is attested in 1908.

## Nebulous

A 'nebulous' answer to a question would lack precision and definition, in much the same way as a cloud appears indistinct in the sky, changing with every second and defying all attempts to capture its outline with anything approaching the slightest degree of accuracy. And this explains the derivation of the word.

It found its way into English in the fourteenth century from the Latin *nebulosus*, 'misty' or 'foggy', which is cognate with the Greek words *nephos* (νέφος) and *nephelē* (νεφέλη), both of which meant 'cloud'. Interestingly, the Greek words are related to the Russian *nebo*, meaning 'sky'.

## Neurotic

The term 'neurotic', both as an adjective and as a noun, has featured in English since the late nineteenth century and essentially describes a person suffering from a neurosis, such as excessive anxiety. The derivative Greek noun *neuron* (νεῦρον) meant 'a nerve', although it was also the word for 'sinew' and 'tendon'. In a metaphorical sense it was also used by the Ancient Greeks to refer to vigour or strength, in much the same way as we might refer to a strong character as having the 'nerve' to engage in risky or perhaps even life-threatening pursuits. And then, of course, if a person's moral fibre is unequal to the task, we can say that they have 'lost their nerve'.

Interestingly, the Greeks also used the term for the string on an archery bow and the chord on a musical instrument, which might account for the English expression 'highly strung'.

The same root has given us words such as *neuralgia* (pain affecting the nervous system), *neurology* (a study of the nervous system) and *neurasthenia* (a lack of energy or vigour).

# Nike

There can be few people in the world who are unfamiliar with the word 'Nike'. The trademark logo emblazons what is probably the most famous sporting footwear ever manufactured (the company was founded in the USA in 1964). It is worth mentioning, however, that the correct pronunciation does not rhyme with 'mike' but is really two syllables and should sound like 'nee-kay'.

The trade name 'Nike' is adopted from the Greek *nikē* (νίκη), 'victory'. When personified and spelled with a capital letter, Nikē (Νίκη) was the goddess of victory in Ancient Greece and the counterpart of the Roman goddess Victoria. The company logo (known as

a 'swoosh') is intended to create an impression of speed and at the same time represent the goddess's wings.

In addition to victory, Nikē was the goddess of strength and speed, who in Greek mythology assumed the role of a charioteer, charging about the battlefield, picking out those who had fought valiantly and slain their enemies. She then bestowed upon them laurel leaves, symbolizing the glory and fame to which their courage and valour entitled them.

But the influence of Nikē does not end there. Her name lies at the root of modern forenames such as Nicholas, Nicola and, in slightly more obscure forms, Berenice and Veronica. The last two are merely variations of the Greek *Pherenikē* (Φερένικη), 'the bringer of victory'.

# Noise

Believe it or not, it is thought that this word can trace its history all the way back to the Ancient Greek for a 'ship'. It has been used in English since the thirteenth century to define an unpleasant sound; prior to that it was more associated with sea-sickness and the Latin word *nausea*. But the Latin word was derived from the Greek *nausía* (ναυσία), 'seasickness', the awful feeling experienced by those tossed about in a *naus* (ναῦς), or ship. No doubt somebody at some stage realized that a terrible din can make a person feel sick just as much as a bad sea crossing can.

# Nomad

People who traditionally, either by circumstance or choice, lead a life of wandering from place to place, as opposed to the settled existence enjoyed by the majority of the Earth's population, have been known as 'nomads' in English since the mid-sixteenth century.

The derivation of the word is the Greek *nomos* (νομός), 'pasture land'; the original 'nomads', or *nomades* (νομάδεσ) in Greek, were shepherds who wandered around looking for suitable, richly grassed areas where they could graze their flocks. The associated verb here is *nemein* (νέμειν), 'to allot'; the land where the sheep or cattle grazed would have been 'allotted' or 'set aside' for the purpose.

But there is an interesting link here with another Greek work frequently used in English: *nemesis* (νέμεσις). As a common noun the Greek word meant 'indignation', 'anger at injustice' and the vengeance likely to be exacted by the gods for intemperate or inconsiderate behaviour. When personified, Nemesis (Νέμεσις) was also the goddess of retribution, bringing down those who experienced good fortune undeservedly.

## Nostalgia

The way we use this word in modern English (actually only since 1920) reflects a slight change of emphasis from the spatial to the temporal when compared with the original Greek. We use it to describe that dreamy feeling of wishing to return to former times when life was simpler (and supposedly better), but the word is a seventeenth-century construction from *nostos* (νόστος), 'a return home', and *algos* (ἄλγος), 'pain', 'grief', 'sorrow'. So, a more accurate translation of the Greek would be along the lines of 'the pain experienced by a person who is desperately homesick'.

## Nymphomania

As a term first used in English in the eighteenth century to describe a medical condition in women characterized by an unusually strong sex drive, the word comprises *numphē* (νύμφη), 'nymph', a marriageable young woman or bride, and the suffix *mania* (μᾰνίᾱ), 'mania'.

In Greek mythology the word 'nymph' was also applied to creatures who differed greatly from marriageable young women on the threshold of blissful wedlock. These were the fairy-like beings, the daughters of Zeus, who came down from Heaven in a shower of rain and inhabited the woods, rivers and other places of natural calm and beauty. They were not considered immortal, but were reputed to enjoy long, playful lives. The most important of them were:

| | |
|---|---|
| *Dryads* | lived among the trees, especially oaks |
| *Hamadryads* | died at the same time as their host tree |
| *Oreads* | inhabited the mountains |
| *Kranides* | the nymphs of the springs |
| *Meliades* | the nymphs of fruit trees (particularly apples) |
| *Alsēides* | the nymphs of the groves and glades |

## Ocean

The poet Hesiod maintained that Ōkeanos (Ὠκεανός) was the son of *Ouranos* (Οὐρανός), Heaven, and *Gaia* (Γαῖα), Earth, and – far from being the vast masses of water we associate with the term today – was a river encompassing the whole Earth and from which all other waterways (rivers, streams, seas etc.) were derived.

The word 'ocean' made its way into English in the thirteenth century from the Old French *occean*, borrowed from the Latin *oceanus*. Until *c*.1650 the more usual term was 'ocean sea' (a direct translation of the Latin *mare oceanum*); it was not until the fourteenth century that individual bodies of water were called 'oceans'.

One theory is that the word is derived from *ōkus* (ὠκύς), 'swift', and the verb *naō* (νάω), 'I flow', suggesting that Homer's term *ōkeanos potamos* (ὠκεανὸς ποταμός) possibly means 'fast-flowing river'. However, there is currently no commonly agreed etymology.

## Optician

'Optician' is used in the UK as a catch-all expression for the high-street practitioner we visit when we find we are not seeing things as well as we used to. The title is derived from the Greek *optikos* (ὀπτικος), 'pertaining to the eye', from the Greek *ops* (ὄψ), 'eye', and related to the verb *optuein* (ὀπτευειν), 'to see'.

An optician is just one of several professionals involved in community eye care, being, strictly speaking, a technician trained in the design and fitting of lenses according to a prescription provided by an optometrist. This is a specialist who examines a patient's eyes and calculates the dimensions of the lenses required to correct his or her vision. The word is a combination of the Greek for 'eye' and the word *metron* (μέτρον), 'measurement'.

## THE CYCLOPES

In Greek mythology the Cyclopes were a particularly unpleasant race of giants whose dominant physical feature was a single, round eye (*kuklos*, 'circle'; *ops*, 'eye') in the middle of their forehead. Tradition had it that they lived in the depths of the volcano Mount Etna and slaved away all day for Hephaestos, the god of blacksmiths. They were led by one Polyphemos, who, according to Homer, was tricked and blinded by Odysseus during the course of his wanderings.

But this account was not the only one. The poet Hesiod identified three Cyclopes: Argēs, the flashing bright light; Steropēs, lightning; Brontēs, thunder. According to the poet this delightful trio fashioned the thunderbolts that Zeus was so fond of hurling down on defenceless mortals, as well as the Helmet of Invisibility worn by Hades, the god of the underworld. They also forged the trident brandished with such panache by Poseidon, the god of the oceans and earthquakes.

# *Orchestra*

The meaning we attach to this word today – a group of musicians producing sweet music – has only existed since the early eighteenth century. The original Greek word *orchēstra* (ὀρχήστρα) was a semi-circular space where a group of dancers performed as they commented on the action of the play being enacted in front of the audience.

The related verb was *orchesthai* (ὀρχεῖσθαι), 'to rise up'. The original meaning of the noun, therefore, was a place where people 'stood up' and started to dance – that is, a dance floor.

## Orphan

The word 'orphan' has been used in English since about 1300 to define a child bereft of both parents. It entered the language via Late Latin, which had *orphanus*, borrowed from the Greek *orphanos* (ὀρφανός) with the same meaning. The literal meaning of the Greek is really 'deprived of', so its application to children 'deprived of' their fathers and mothers is an understandable development. However, for the Greeks, a child could be described as *orphanos* if he or she had been left just without a father.

It is also directly related to a Latin adjective *orbus*, which also meant 'orphan' but had the additional meaning of 'destitute'. The linguistic association between being orphaned and suffering severe economic misfortune tells us much about the lack of social care available to the unfortunate in the ancient world.

## Orthodox

Since the sixteenth century this word has been used in English to describe ideas, thoughts and opinions that do not differ from those of the majority. In a religious context it is an adjective that has been applied to the eastern branches of Christianity (i.e. Greek Orthodox, Russian Orthodox) since the eighteenth century. Orthodox Judaism is a definition that was coined in 1853.

It is a combination of two Greek words, the first being *orthos* (ὀρθός), meaning basically 'straight' but with the extended meanings of 'true', 'real' or 'correct'. The second is *doxa* (δόξᾰ), 'thinking' or 'opinion', from the verb *dokein* (δοκεῖν), 'to think'. When the two elements are combined the result is an adjective that basically means 'straight thinking' or 'of the correct opinion'.

Anybody, of course, who is not 'of the correct opinion' is described as holding 'heterodox' views. Here we have the same noun with a different prefix, *hetero* (ἕτερος), 'other', 'different', giving us a compound adjective that simply means 'of a different opinion'.

## Ostracize

In the modern world if a person is ostracized by society he or she is ignored, shunned or simply not permitted to take part in social, commercial or public activities. In ancient Athens, however, 'ostracism' involved banishment of ten years from the city and, depending on the age of the person so condemned, could mean that he or she died far from his or her native soil.

The word is derived from the Greek *ostrakismos* (ὀστρακισμός), which referred to a system of banishment executed by writing the selected person's name on a potsherd or earthenware tile known as an *ostrakon* (ὄστρακον). If enough people wrote the same name on one of these bits of hardened clay, the person concerned had no choice but to pack his or her bags and leave. An *ostrakon* was so called because it was usually made of sun-baked clay and was as hard as a piece of bone, the Greek for which was *osteon* (ὀστέον).

But the Greeks also applied the term *ostrakon* (ὄστρακον) to the bone-hard shells of creatures such as snails and tortoises as well as the *ostreon* (ὄστρεον), which we now recognize as an 'oyster'. And it is also, of course, the derivation of many medical terms referring to conditions of the bones and beginning with the prefix 'osteo-'.

## Oxymoron

This word is loosely used in modern English as a synonym for a 'contradiction in terms' – although, strictly speaking, to qualify as an oxymoron a contradiction in terms has to comprise words that are directly opposite in meaning, such as 'bitter-sweet', 'foolishly wise' or 'repulsively attractive'. It was a rhetorical technique, the term for which entered English in the seventeenth century when public speakers realized that its use could lend added impact to what they were saying.

The word 'oxymoron' (itself an oxymoron) was used by the Ancient Greeks, who described anyone who was not particularly intelligent as *oxymoros* (ὀξύμωρος), 'pointedly foolish'. The two components of the word were *oxus* (ὀξύς), 'sharp', and *mōros* (μῶρος), 'blunt', 'dull' or 'stupid'.

## Ozone

Ever since the 1970s people the world over have been warned about the harmful effects of the hole in the 'ozone layer', a mass of gas hovering in the stratosphere and protecting animal and plant life on Earth from the Sun's harmful ultraviolet rays.

The word was coined by the German chemist Christian Friedrich Schönbein in 1839. He noticed that after a lighting strike the air was filled with a strange, pungent smell which he could not identify, and so decided to invent a name for it himself. Like many scientists before and after him, he turned to Ancient Greek and found the verb *ozein* (ὄζειν), 'to give off a smell' (pleasant or unpleasant), from which he formed the German noun *Ozon*. This became the English 'ozone'.

A very close relative of the word 'ozone' is 'odour'. This entered English in the thirteenth century, from the Old French and Latin *odor*, related to the Greek *odmē* (ὀδμή), also derived from the verb *ozein*.

The somewhat literary phrase 'odour of sanctity' has been used in English since the mid-eighteenth century. It is a borrowing of the French expression *odeur de sainteté*, derived from the ancient belief that the corpses of well-known saints gave off a particularly sweet smell or odour either at the point of death or later, if for some reason the body had to be exhumed.

## Panacea

This word appeared in English in or around 1510 as *panace*, but by the 1540s it was being spelled 'panacea' to reflect the Latin *panacea*, the name for a herb which, in the ancient world, was believed to be a cure-all for just about every illness known to mankind.

The word was originally a Greek noun *panakeia* (πανάκεια), comprising two elements, *pan* (πᾶν), 'all', and *akos* (ἄκος), 'cure', 'remedy', 'relief'. Putting both elements together produced the word for virtually any compound, plant or substance that, the Greeks believed, was an antidote for all disease

## Pandora's box

A rather literary turn of phrase (first used in English in the 1570s), frequently applied to almost any venture or activity best avoided as it might well lead to more unforeseen problems than could possibly be anticipated. 'Opening a can of worms' is a relatively modern equivalent.

According to Greek myth, Pandora was the first woman on Earth and took her name from two Greek words, *pan* (πᾶν), 'all', and *dōra* (δῶρα), 'gifts', so she was really the woman who 'had all the gifts'. Prometheus, we learn, stole fire from the gods and gave it to the mortals. When Zeus heard about this he was consumed with rage and commanded his blacksmith, Hephaestos, to make a woman out of earth and water. When the basic model was ready, the other gods all contributed a gift each until the final product was ready for despatch down to Earth. Aphrodite bestowed beauty on her; the Graces gave her gold ribbon; Peitho gave her spring flowers; and Hermēs made her bold and cunning. These, and gifts from other gods, were intended to make Pandora a wily seductress who would bring misery to men and eventually cause their downfall.

But, in addition, she was given a 'box' containing all the ills that could destroy man's idyllic happiness and life of pure bliss. She was ordered to bring this down to Earth but not to open it, an instruction she forgot. So, once among the mortals, where she married Epimetheus, Prometheus' brother, she opened the box and out flew pain, sickness and death and a few other unwelcome gifts for mankind. Pandora, however, suddenly remembered that she was not supposed to open the box and slammed the lid shut. But she was too late and almost all the contents had escaped; the only remaining 'gift', which she managed to trap inside the box, was Hope. Humankind was now doomed to perpetual torment, the only consolation being the knowledge that Pandora's box still contained Hope and therefore the possibility that, at some time in the future, things would improve.

## LOST IN TRANSLATION

According to the original Greek version, Pandora's 'box' was not a box at all. It appears that the Dutch scholar Erasmus (*c*.1466–1536) confused two Greek words when he was translating Hesiod's account, in which the woes visited upon humankind were kept in a large earthenware wine jar or *pithos*. Erasmus misread this as *puxis*, 'box', and the mistake was never corrected.

# *Panic*

In Ancient Greece everybody believed in gods. All human activities and emotions were regulated and overseen by some god or other. One of these gods was Pan (Πάν), who dwelt among the forests and woodland outside the major Greek towns and was capable of striking fear into unsuspecting passers-by. This particular type of terror came to be known as *panikon deima* (πανικὸν δεῖμα), 'the fear caused by Pan'. This was abbreviated in English to 'panic'.

When the word first entered English in the seventeenth century it meant nothing more than 'relating to Pan'. In the same century, however, it gradually came to refer to contagious emotional reaction spreading through a group; finally, in the eighteenth century, it acquired the meaning we attach to it today – sudden alarm.

## Panoply

Used mainly now as an expression synonymous with 'the full set of' or 'the full array of', the word 'panoply' has its roots in the endless wars the Ancient Greeks seemed to have been involved in.

The basic derivative noun is *hoplon* (ὅπλον), which could mean any tool or implement, but in a military context was the heavy shield carried by the ordinary foot soldier. In the plural, *hopla* (ὅπλα) was a general word covering the implements of war, including armour, harnesses and so on. And if an ordinary soldier was fortunate enough to be able to afford a complete set of protective armour, this was referred to as his *panoplia* (πανοπλία) and consisted of a shield, sword, breastplate and/or a spear.

When 'panoply' was first used in English in the six-teenth century it had a spiritual rather than a military significance. By the seventeenth it was used in a military context as a complete suit of armour. Its use in a purely non-military context, suggesting simply a 'vast array of', dates from 1829.

## Panto

Panto – or, to give it its full name, pantomime – has been a feature of the English theatre since the seventeenth century. In the 1610s a 'pantomime' was a mime actor – someone who performed on stage using gestures and movement but no speech. By 1735 the term was applied to the drama or play, but the essential ingredient was still total silence on the part of the actors.

The origin of the word is Greek. The first part of the word, 'panto', is from the word *pan* (πᾶν), 'all'; 'mime' is an adaptation of the Greek *mimēsis* (μίμησις), 'imitation', from the verb *mimeisthai* (μιμεῖσθαι), 'to imitate', also the origin of the more modern verb 'to mimic'. When the constituent parts are assembled the result is the Greek *pantomimos* (παντόμιμος), meaning 'an imitator of all'.

Of course, the only time most of us come across this word now is at Christmas time when families tradition-ally flock to their local theatres to watch men dressed as women, and a principal 'boy' who is always an attractive woman, and to listen to rather bawdy jokes and songs and observe the antics of a host of stock characters. This type of performance has been enjoyed by generations since 1739; it is far removed from the silent productions of a century earlier.

## Paradise

If we want to have some idea of the derivation of this word we must rid our minds of all preconceived ideas about a state of perfection where all is calm and serenity and where existence is nothing but endless joy, contentment and bliss. The real meaning of the word is far more down to earth, quite literally.

Ultimately, it is an Old Iranian word and is believed to have been introduced to Europe by the Greek historian, soldier and adventurer Xenophon. When the Greeks acquired it, they manipulated it a little to fit in with their language; a little more manipulation produced the form we recognize in English today.

The Old Iranian form was *pairidaeza*, meaning literally no more than a walled enclosure or parkland. The Greek version of this was a combination of *peri* (περί), 'around', and *teichos* (τεῖχος), 'wall', giving *periteichismos* (περιτεχισμός), 'a surrounding wall', and the verb *periteichizein* (περιτειχίζειν), 'to build a wall around'. And the associated noun *paradeisos* (παράδεισος) was used at this time by the Greeks to designate the carefully cultivated parklands belonging to the Persian nobles and king and walled off from the rest of the people. By the time of the New Testament, *paradeisos* (παράδεισος) was being used as a synonym for Heaven (the abode of the blessed); it was adopted into English in the twelfth century (via Latin *paradisus* and Old French *paradis*) with the same meaning.

The spiritual definition is perhaps comforting, but there is no escaping the fact that the original meaning of 'paradise' was nothing more than an area of land 'with a wall built around it'.

## Paragon

The Ancient Greeks, as we know, were no strangers to war. And war in those days meant close-quarter, hand-to-hand fighting and the use of some fairly fearsome weapons such as spears, swords and axes.

When preparing for war the soldiers of Athens, Sparta and a dozen other city states would have spent hours honing their arrows, knives and swords on what we refer to today as a 'whetstone' in order to produce as sharp a point as possible. The Greek for a point was *akis* (ἀκίς); the whetstone was an *akonē* (ἀκόνη); and the associated verb, 'to sharpen', was *akonan* (ἀκονᾶν). The addition of the prefix *para-* (παρα-) gave *parakonan* (παρακονᾶν), 'to sharpen something against something else' – in this case a knife, sword or arrowhead against the whetstone.

Early in the fourteenth century the word was adopted by the Italians, who used a *paragone*, 'touchstone', when testing the purity of gold and other precious metals. When it appeared in English in the 1540s, anglicized as 'paragon', it meant a 'model of excellence' against which everything else could be compared (interestingly, modern Italian still has *paragone* for 'comparison' and *paragonare* for 'to compare').

The idea of a 'paragon' as a standard of excellence against which others were measured was eventually applied also to people. This explains why we can now describe somebody as a 'paragon of virtue' if we wish to single out a particular man or woman against whose moral standards those of others should be judged.

A highly specialized use of the word occurs in the world of gemmology where a 'paragon' is a perfect diamond of 100 carats or more.

## Paragraph

In the sixteenth century, when printing in Europe was becoming ever more widespread, the word *paragraphe* appeared in French, borrowed from the Medieval Latin *paragraphus*, denoting a passage or particular section of a book. But a new 'paragraph' was denoted by a horizontal stroke written either beneath the beginning of the new section or in the margin, alongside the text. And this is the best indicator of the origin of the word.

'Paragraph' is taken from the Greek *paragraphē* (παρα–γραφή), 'a marginal note', and the verb *paragraphein* (παραγράφειν), meaning 'to write alongside', 'to add in writing'.

Over time the custom of writing paragraph markers, when there was a change in sense or the argument of the written passage took a different direction, gave way to the current practice wherein the first line of the new 'paragraph' is usually indented. In the printing trade paragraphs were traditionally indicated by a special mark known as a 'pilcrow'.

## Paranoid

Strictly speaking, this is a word which should remain in the realm of psychiatry, but it has found its way into common parlance, applied loosely to anyone who is believed, rightly or wrongly, to imagine that people are talking about them. It was first used with its modern spelling in English in 1848, but was known as early as 1811 with the spelling 'paranoea'.

With the advent of psychiatry as a recognized branch of science the word was borrowed directly from the Greek *paranoia* (παράνοια), meaning 'mental derangement', 'madness', 'folly'. It comprised the prefix *para-* (παρά-), 'against', 'beyond', 'contrary to', and the noun *nous* (νοῦς), 'mind'. So, what the medical world defines as a chronic disturbance of the mind characterized by delusions of grandeur and a persecution mania is, etymologically speaking, basically a mind behaving in a manner contrary to the way it is supposed to behave.

*psuchēs megas chalinos estin ho noos*

ψυχῆς μέγας χαλινός ἐστιν ὁ νόος

'the mind is a great bridle for the soul'

MENANDER


## Paraphernalia

We now apply this word to miscellaneous items or belongings which perhaps serve no obvious purpose. The original meaning, however, was very different and far more precise. It entered English in the seventeenth century from Medieval Latin, which had *paraphernalia*, a borrowing and adaptation of the original Greek *parapherna* (παράφερνα), the belongings and property a bride brought to a marriage in addition to the dowry and which the law allowed the bride to regard as her own property. Its application to miscellaneous items dates from the eighteenth century.

The word comprises two elements: *para* (παρά), 'alongside', and *phernē* (φερνή), 'that which has been brought', or more specifically a dowry, derived from the verb *pherein* (φέρειν), 'to bring', 'to carry'.

## Parasite

The implication behind this word as it is now used is always one of deliberate dependence on someone else or, at least, of benefiting from another's endeavours. And this is not all that far removed from the original Greek. The noun *sitos* (σῖτος), 'grain', 'corn', and then 'food', generally, but particularly 'bread', was combined with the prefix *para* (παρά), 'alongside', to produce *parasitos* (παράσιτος), 'someone who sits alongside and feeds off another man's table'.

The word 'parasite' was absorbed into English in the sixteenth century and applied to people who obtained hospitality by fawning and being obsequious. In the eighteenth century it was adopted into the world of science and applied to plants and animals relying on the support of others for their very existence.

# Parliament

Very early in the fourteenth century the word 'parliament' was used in English to denote a formal conference. Later in the same century it was the term used to describe the Great Council of the Realm, which of course is how we understand the word today.

Its immediate antecedent is the Old French *parlement*, an eleventh-century word derived from the verb *parler*, 'to speak'. And *parlement* was related to the Anglo-Latin *parliamentum*, attested in the early thirteenth century.

If we now trace the history of *parler* as far back as Late Latin we find the verb *parabolare*, 'to speak', and the associated noun *parabola*, 'speech', 'discourse'. And this is where we detect a slight variation of meaning; *parabola* existed in Latin, but meant 'comparison', which is precisely the sense of the derivative Greek noun *parabolē* (παραβολή).

The associated verb was *paraballein* (παραβάλλειν), a compound of *para* (παρά), 'alongside', and *ballein* (βάλλειν), 'to throw'. The basic idea here is that one object could be 'thrown alongside another' for the purposes of comparison. In the abstract sense this could also apply to a story which might serve to illustrate a moral point or as an allegory to convey a spiritual message. Therefore the lexical combination that gave us the word 'parliament' also gave us the word 'parable', but via very different routes.

# Pathetic

When this adjective entered English in the late sixteenth century it was used as a synonym for 'having an effect on the emotions'. It gradually changed in meaning until, by the 1930s, it had acquired the unflattering connotations we associate with it today: 'ridiculous', 'pretty bad', 'not arousing admiration'.

The basic idea of the original Greek noun from which the word is derived centred around suffering. The verb *pathein* (παθεῖν), a form of the verb *paschein* (πάσχειν) meant 'to suffer'; its related adjective *pathētikos* (παθητικός) was used to describe people whom we would think of as 'sensitive' or who have difficulty concealing their feelings.

The Greek adjective *apathēs* (ἀπαθής) meant 'free from suffering' and produced the English term 'apathetic'. Originally this would have had the same meaning as the Ancient Greek, but by the eighteenth century it had acquired the meaning we attach to it today: 'indifferent'. Presumably, people who are 'indifferent' to events are unlikely to 'suffer' because of them.

Other words associated with the Greek for 'suffering' include: sympathy ('feeling with'), empathy ('in a state of emotion') and telepathy ('feeling at a distance').

# Period

This word is now mainly used in English to denote the distance between two points in time, but the Greek word from which it is derived had spatial as well as chronological connotations.

The word *periodos* (περίοδος) comprised two elements: *peri* (περί), 'around', and *hodos* (ὁδός), 'way', 'path', 'journey'. Its basic meaning was therefore 'travelling around', 'journey around', and so eventually came to mean 'a round trip', 'a circuit' and even, in the world of grammar and writing, a complete sentence. By extension, it also came to define a traveller's account of his journeys as well as the indispensable piece of equipment for any wanderer, a map.

When the word was absorbed into English in the fourteenth century it was spelled 'parodie' (not to be confused with parody); this did not change into the form that we recognize today until the sixteenth century.

The concept of 'a length of time' evolved from the word's basic meaning of a 'cycle of events' with a specific beginning and end.

## Pharmacy

A place where drugs are sold or distributed has been referred to as a 'pharmacy' only since the first half of the nineteenth century. Prior to that, the word was used to define the art of preparing and mixing various drugs in order to produce whatever medicine was needed at the time. In the thirteenth century the French version of the word, *farmacie*, meant specifically 'a purgative'.

The Greek word from which the modern form is thought to have derived is *pharmakon* (φάρμακον), meaning almost any compound from a drug or potion to a deadly poison. A man who administered such concoctions was known as a *pharmakeus* (φαρμάκευς), 'a purveyor of drugs and poisons' – but in Ancient Greece the dividing line between medicine and magic was frequently somewhat blurred, so he could also be a 'sorcerer'.

A derivative verb *pharmakeuein* (φαρμαχεύειν) was 'to administer drugs'; its associated adjective (*pharmakeutikos*) (φαρμάκευτικός), 'relating to drugs', provided the modern English 'pharmaceutical'.

## Pheasant

In the part of the world the Ancient Greeks referred to as Colchis, but which we know as the country of Georgia, there flows a river now known as either the Rioni or the Rion. To the Ancient Greeks this was the *Phasis* (Φᾶσις), and the surrounding area was renowned as the habitat of a species of brightly coloured birds that bred there in great numbers. Having no other name for the bird, the Greeks simply referred to it as the *phasianos ornis* (φασιανος ὄρνις), 'the Phasis bird'.

This term was adopted by the Romans, who abbreviated it to *phasianus*, which subsequently found its way into Old French as *faisan* and then into Norman French as *feasaunt* (the 't' was added in error); by the thirteenth century it had reached English and was being spelled as it is today.

## Phlegm

Considering the cold sticky nature of the gooey substance referred to here it is rather strange that the word comes from the Greek verb *phlegein* (φλέγειν), 'to burn', and *phlegma* (φλέγμα), principally a medical term meaning 'flame', 'heat'. The apparent contradiction is explained by the medieval belief that although the mucous was cold and slimy it was a reaction to bodily heat. And when the body was so overheated that it produced an excessive amount of phlegm it caused the person afflicted to become listless and weary, or, as we would now say, 'phlegmatic'.

The word has been used in English since the fourteenth century but its modern spelling has only been around since the 1660s.

## Phobia

Now used frequently as an alternative for the word 'fear', 'phobia' is a direct borrowing from the Greek *phobos* (φόβος). In Greek mythology this word was personified as Phobos (Φόβος), the son of Arēs (Ἄρης), the god of war, and brother of Deimos (Δεῖμος), 'terror'. According to Greek legend, Phobos and Deimos always accompanied their father into battle.

It is possible to make up as many 'phobias' as we want simply by combining a Greek word with the suffix -phobia. Here are a few:

| | |
|---:|:---|
| *acrophobia* | fear of heights |
| *agoraphobia* | fear of open spaces (lit. marketplaces) |
| *ailurophobia* | fear of cats |
| *amathophobia* | fear of dust |
| *arachnophobia* | fear of spiders |
| *cynophobia* | fear of dogs |
| *hydrophobia* | fear of water |
| *phobophobia* | fear of being afraid |
| *photophobia* | fear of the light |
| *skotophobia* | fear of the dark |
| *tokophobia* | fear of childbirth |
| *xenophobia* | fear of foreigners |

## Physics

Words such as 'physics', 'physical', 'physique', and even 'metaphysical', all share a common origin: the Greek word *phusis* (φύσις), 'nature'.

In thirteenth-century English the word *fusike* meant 'the art of healing' (which accounts for the popularity of 'physic gardens' where herbs and plants were grown for their healing properties), borrowed from the Old French *fisike*, 'natural science', 'the art of healing'. But both the English and French words had been taken directly from the Latin, which had *physica*, 'the study of nature', closely reflecting the original Greek expression *phusikē*

## THE METAPHYSICALS

The word 'metaphysical' has been subjected to misunderstanding ever since it was first borrowed from the Greeks. Samuel Johnson famously coined the phrase in relation to those we now think of as the metaphysical poets (Donne, Herbert, Marvell, etc.), basing his choice of word on the fact that the poets concerned frequently used complicated literary conceits, particularly 'metaphors', with which he mistakenly associated the word 'metaphysical'.

An earlier error involved Latin scholars who misinterpreted Andronicus of Rhodes, a Greek philosopher of the first century BCE who edited the works of Aristotle. Andronicus arranged Aristotle's writings in a particular order, starting with 'First Philosophy', followed by 'Physics'. Everything else he organized as 'the books coming after Physics', the Greek for which is *ta meta ta phusika biblia* (τὰ μετὰ τὰ φυσικὰ βιβλία). Later commentators took this to mean 'books dealing with what is beyond nature', a misconception that has survived down the ages.

*epistemē* (φυσικὴ ἐπιστήμη), 'understanding of nature'. This expression was derived from the noun *phusis* (φύσις), 'nature', and the verb *phuein* (φύειν), 'to bring forth', 'to produce', 'to cause to be'. By the 1580s 'physics' was the term used to denote the study of natural sciences; by the early eighteenth century it defined the study of matter and energy, as it still does today.

# Pirate

In modern parlance we frequently use this word to denote somebody who makes unauthorized use of another's artistic work – in effect a synonym for 'thief'. It has been a common term since the very early eighteenth century for somebody who robs the artistic endeavours of another, but previously it was almost always associated in English with robbery at sea.

The abstract noun 'piracy' evolved in the fifteenth century and by the 1570s the verb 'to pirate' had also made its appearance. The concrete noun 'pirate', however, had been used in English since about 1300. It made its way into English from the Latin *pirata*, 'a plunderer of ships', 'a corsair', but the Greek noun from which the word was derived had evolved from a very innocuous verb. The noun was *peiratēs* (πειρατής), latterly a 'sea robber' but originally simply 'someone who makes an attempt'. The associated verb *peiran* (πειρᾶν) meant nothing more than 'to try one's hand at', 'to attempt' or even 'to try one's luck'. So, when we boil it down to basics, Captain Hook and Long John Silver of the novels of yesteryear might have been cut-throats and brigands, but they were also simply men 'willing to have a go'.

# Place

The Old English for what we would now think of as a 'place' was *stow* or *stede* (alternatively *stead*), surviving in place names such as Stow-on-the-Wold and Berkhamsted, and in words such as 'farmstead', 'homestead' and the phrase 'instead of'. In the twelfth century this was replaced, under the influence of Norman French, by the word *place* (which had been acquired by the French from the medieval Latin *placea*), a term applied to a broad street resembling more a village or town square than simply a specific spot where something is situated. If we remember cognate nouns in modern European languages such as Italian *piazza*, Spanish *plaza* and the German *Platz*, all of which retain the idea of a 'square' surrounded by buildings of one sort or another, we see that they are closer in meaning to the original Norman French.

By the fourteenth century the word in English meant 'an inhabited area' and by the 1580s it referred to a group of houses within a town. But it was also in the fourteenth century that the meaning widened so that the word could refer to a particular spot or situation, or even a 'place' in a book. In the sixteenth century it was applied figuratively to the position or office a person occupied within an organization.

All these meanings can trace their origin back to a single Greek word, *platus* (πλατύς), meaning 'flat' or 'broad'. The association with the layout of a town arose from the Greek term *plateia hodos* (πλατεῖα ὁδός), literally 'a broad way or street'.

Just to complete the picture, we might also point out that the fish known in English as a 'plaice', spelled *plaise* or *plaiz* when it entered English in the thirteenth century, is from the same Greek adjective. After all, it is also recognized by its 'flat', or 'broad', appearance.

## Plaster

The sticky strip of material we reach for if we cut our finger and the mixture we spread across a brick wall before painting it share a common origin. The Ancient Greeks knew that the best way to staunch a bleeding wound was to smear it with a gluey preparation, in much the same way that, since the fourteenth century, builders have been daubing walls to form a base on which to paint.

The medical preparation in Ancient Greece was known as *emplastron* (ἔμπλαστρον), formed from *en-* (ἐν-), 'on', and *plastos* (πλαστός), 'moulded', 'shaped'. This in turn was a derivative of the verb *plassein* (πλάσσειν), 'to mould'.

The basic, original idea for 'plaster' in both senses, then, was 'to daub', 'to spread', a flexible substance over a particular area.

Also derived from the same linguistic root are words such as 'plastic' and the clay substitute invented in 1879 and known by the trade name Plasticine.

## Pneumonia

The term for the serious medical condition affecting the lungs is first recorded in English in the seventeenth century. The root of the noun is the Greek verb *pnein* (πνέιν), 'to breathe', and various associated nouns all connected in some way with breathing. The noun *pneumōn* (πνεύμων) meant 'lung'; another noun, *pneuma* (πνεῦμα), had a quite varied set of meanings – it could refer to air or wind, breath and, in a religious context, the spirit. It was also personified in the ecclesiastical expression *hagion Pneuma* (ἅγιον Πνεῦμα), 'the Holy Spirit'.

Also connected is the word 'pneumatic', as in a 'pneumatic drill', which is basically just a tool operated by air.

## Poet

If we remember that in medieval Britain the composer of songs and verses was frequently known as a 'maker', we have a good indication of the derivation of the word. In Ancient Greece a *poiētēs* (ποιητής), 'poet', was a person who could compose a *poiēma* (ποίημα), 'poem', whenever the occasion demanded. Both nouns are derived from the basic verb *poiein* (ποιεῖν), 'to make'. The practice of composing poetry was known to the Ancient Greeks as *poiētikē technē* (ποιητική τέχνη), 'the poetic art', 'the poetic skill'.

The Greek term was absorbed into English in the early fourteenth century.

# Pole

There is no 'pole' protruding from the snow and ice at either the North Pole or the South Pole; the explanation of why we insist on referring to them lies with the Greeks. In the fourteenth century the word was adopted into English to define each of two points in the celestial sphere. In the sixteenth century the word was used to refer to the ends of an imaginary axis running from north to south through the centre of the Earth. In the same century, 'pole' was adopted as the term for the end of a bar magnet.

The origin of the word in these contexts is the Greek *polos* (πόλος), 'axis', a derivative of the verb *pelein* (πέλειν), 'to move', 'to revolve'.

# Politics

The Greek word for an independent, self-governing community such as Athens or Sparta was *polis* (πόλις), 'city state'. The word has filtered down into English in several guises. The derivative *politēs* (πολίτης), for instance, 'someone who lived in a *polis*', was the Greek equivalent of our 'citizen', and the study of how such citizens should behave and be governed was known to the Ancient Greeks as *politikē tekhnē* (πολιτική τέχνη). This could be translated as 'the art of living in a city state', or more simply 'political science'. The associated plural noun *politika* (πολιτικά), 'the things to do with the *polis*', is the origin of the modern English word 'politics'. It is also the origin of the word 'politician' (literally, 'someone who concerns himself with the affairs of the *polis*'), which entered English in the sixteenth century. It should be pointed out, however, that at that time it was also synonymous with 'schemer' or 'intriguer'!

Citizens and politicians, of course, need to be protected so that they can go about their daily business, sure in the knowledge that, as they do so, there is a body of men whose task it is to protect them from miscreants and criminals. And such a force has been known in Britain since the eighteenth century as 'the police'. The term has spread so far throughout the world now that it is easy to forget that, in essence, it refers to officers of the law protecting law-abiding citizens in what Socrates, Plato and Aristophanes would have referred to as a *polis*.


## Pompous

Many descriptive phrases accompany the adjective 'pompous', such as 'full of himself', 'likes the sound of her own voice', 'puts on airs and graces', and so on. The adjective, then, is suggestive of a person who attempts to give the impression that he or she is far more important than is the case.

The origin of the word, however, is quite an ordinary, everyday Greek word: *pempein* (πέμπειν), 'to send'. The associated noun *pompē* (πομπή) at first meant simply 'a sending' or 'an escort', but with the passage of time it came to mean more specifically a procession, perhaps in honour of a god or an escort sent out to accompany a ruler, important politician or leading citizen.

When the Romans picked up the word and converted it into *pompa* it acquired the trappings of splendour and ostentation. No doubt those who took part in such processions dressed to impress and probably felt they deserved the admiration of the crowd, much the same as a 'pompous' person today feels he or she is far more important than those who surround him or her.

In the expression 'pomp and circumstance', the word 'circumstance' reflects an older use of the word meaning 'formality' or 'ceremony'.

'Pomp' and the adjective 'pompous' were first recorded in English in the fourteenth century.

## Porous

A 'porous' material is one which allows moisture and water to seep through. The reason it is able to act in this way is because it is full of microscopic holes or 'pores' acting as a conduit from one side of the material to the other.

The word entered English early in the fourteenth century from Old French, which had the word *poros*, an adaptation of the Medieval Latin adjective *porosus*, from the noun *porus*, 'an opening'.

The Latin, however, was acquired from the Greek *poros* (πόρος), which had several meanings, all reflecting the basic idea of 'movement through or across'. A *poros* could be a 'ford' that wayfarers could use in order to get from one side of a river to the other; it could be a 'way through' a town or city; and it is also related to the modern English 'port', a 'way into or out' of a town, city or country. The derivative Greek verb here was *perān* (περᾶν), 'to drive across or through', 'to let through', 'to traverse'.

The association with Greek has also produced an interesting linguistic phenomenon in other European languages. Several of the Romance languages have more or less the same word for a 'port' and a 'door'. Words for 'port' in French and Spanish are *le port* and *el puerto* respectively, and for 'door' they have *la porte* and *la puerta*. The Portuguese for 'the port' is *o porto* – based on the Latin word *portus*, 'a harbour' – doubling as Porto, the name of the city, which is also the origin of the fortified wine port.

## Pragmatic

In the seventeenth century, when the word entered English, it was rather uncomplimentary to be described as 'pragmatic'. Unlike today, when it implies a business-like approach, in the 1600s it suggested a meddlesome busybody who liked nothing better than to pry into the affairs of others.

The word entered English from French, which had *pragmatique*, a borrowing of the Latin *pragmaticus*, meaning 'skilled in business and law'. The Romans had taken this meaning from the Greek adjective *pragmatikos* (πραγμᾰτικός), meaning all of (i) fit for action or business, (ii) active, (iii) businesslike. But it was applied especially to those who were well versed, and skilled, in affairs of state.

The derivative verb here was *prassein* (πράσσειν), meaning simply 'to do'. Its associated noun *pragma* (πρᾶγμα) had quite a wide range of meanings, including 'business', 'affair', 'fact', 'matter' or, quite simply, 'something to be done'. In its plural form, *pragmata* (πράγματα), it meant 'affairs' or 'circumstances'.

The words 'practical', 'practice', 'practise' and so on are close relatives of 'pragmatic' and share the same Greek origins. But the evolution of their usage is rather complicated and can be confusing, particularly to foreigners who are trying to get to grips with the English language.

The verb 'to practise' appeared in English around the year 1400, meaning more or less the same as 'to do' or 'to act'. A few years later it had acquired the meaning of 'to carry on a profession' and applied particularly, but not exclusively, to the medical profession. This explains why even today we can talk about a doctor or lawyer having a successful 'practice' in the centre of town, but a builder, plumber or double-glazing firm would have an office or a business.

At the same time the noun 'practice' was being used but, certainly in the early part of the fifteenth century, it was being spelled 'practise', no doubt influenced by the Old French *practiser*, simply meaning 'to do' or 'to perform'. Perhaps even more confusingly, it was about this time also that 'to practise' was equated with constant repetition performed by those who wished to acquire a certain level of proficiency or skill in a chosen activity.

The term 'general practitioner' for a family doctor is an interesting one, linguistically speaking. The original term for 'one who does something' was 'practician', a derivative of the Old French *practicien*, a professional person skilled in the law. For some unknown reason, in the 1540s the suffix '-er' was added and the spelling of the word in English settled down as 'practitioner'. A family or community doctor was first described as a 'general practitioner' in 1810.

## Problem

A problem is basically nothing more than a difficulty for which we have not yet found a solution. Another way of thinking about it is to say that something has happened or appeared that is hampering our literal or metaphorical progress in a particular direction. And this is a clue to the origin of the word. The Greek word, from which the English is derived, is *problema* (πρόβλεμα), composed of *pro-* (προ-), 'in front', and *blēmenos* (βλήμενος), 'thrown', from *ballein* (βαλλειν), 'to throw', so that a 'problem' is really just something that has been 'thrown in front of us'.

In the fourteenth century, when the word is first recorded in English, it was synonymous with an enigma or difficult question. It then came to mean 'a matter for discussion'. Finally, in the sixteenth century, it referred to a situation requiring a decision and action leading supposedly to a solution.

## Prophet

Quite apart from its religious contexts, the word 'prophet' can be used now in a secular environment to highlight a person's propensity for telling (or at least attempting to tell) what is going to happen in the future. 'Prophets of doom' are frequently branded as such by those who find their predictions overly pessimistic.

It was a borrowing of the French *prophete*, meaning 'soothsayer', in the twelfth century. This had been acquired from the Latin *propheta*, which in turn was taken from the Greek *prophētēs* (προφήτης), a noun which did not primarily denote a seer who could predict the future. Its basic meaning was a 'spokesman' who represented the views of others or, in a biblical context, one who spoke for God. A 'prophet' was also, in the days of early Christianity, an inspired teacher who took it upon himself to explain or interpret the meaning of the scriptures to others. The idea that a prophet was one who could predict the future appears to have come about through a certain linguistic mix-up.

The Greek prefix *pro-* (προ-) could mean 'before' in both a spatial and temporal context; that is, it could mean 'in front of' or 'prior to'. This means that *prophētēs* (προφήτης) could either define an inspired preacher explaining the will of God 'in front of' a gathering of people, or it could be somebody speaking 'prior to' an event and therefore foretelling it. Further evidence of this can be seen if we consider the related noun, *prophēteia* (προφητεία), 'prophecy', which in Ancient Greece meant either preaching or the gift of foretelling the future.

## Protocol

This word has travelled a long way from its original Greek roots to the meaning we attach to it today. Most people would associate the word now with correct behaviour or etiquette, but in the world of international diplomacy it is also an alternative term for the minutes of a meeting and a formal agreement drawn up between nation-states.

In Medieval Latin its antecedent *protocollum* defined the first sheet of a document on which was recorded the author's name, a list of contents and a note of any corrections contained within the text.

The original idea for such an addition to a manuscript, however, came from Byzantium, where the emperor Justinian the Great (482–565 CE) decreed that all documents should have a flysheet, summarizing the contents, attached to the front for easy reference. And in Byzantium the normal language of communication was Greek, albeit a later variety, and so this page was known as a *prōtokollon* (πρωτόκολλον).

*Prōtokollon* is based on two Greek words, *prōtos* (πρῶτος), 'first', and *kolla* (κόλλα), 'glue', as the original 'protocols' were information sheets 'glued' on to documents as a 'first' page and serving more or less the same function as the table of contents found at the beginning of a modern non-fiction book.

## Psyche

To Homer the *psuchē* (ψυχή) or *psyche* was the soul, spirit or essence of the dead which retained the form of its owner when he or she was alive. It resembles what we would think of as a 'ghost'. For later Greeks it could be any of 'the soul', 'the mind', 'reason' or 'understanding'. It also meant simply 'breath', its associated verb *psuchein* (ψύχειν) being 'to breathe'.

Curiously, however, a *psuchē* (ψυχή) was also a 'butterfly'. The connection seems a little odd until we remember that, to the Greeks, a butterfly emerging from a 'dead' chrysalis symbolized a soul emerging from the body of the recently departed.

The spelling of the word we recognize today has existed in English since the 1640s.

# Pulse

There are two 'pulses' in English: the pulse a doctor takes when he is looking for evidence of a heartbeat, and the edible seed of a leguminous plant. The only thing the two words have in common is that they are both related to Greek.

The 'pulse' we detect in our veins as the blood is pumped around our bodies is related to the Latin *pulsare*, 'to beat', cognate with the Greek *pallein* (πάλλειν), 'to leap', 'to quiver', and another related verb *pelemizein* (πελεμίζειν), 'to quake', 'to tremble'.

On the other hand, the pulses we buy from the greengrocer's shop are related to *poltos* (πόλτος), the Greek for a mushy food similar to what we understand by the word 'porridge'. Another linguistically related word in Greek was *polphos* (πολφός), the dictionary definition of which is 'a farinaceous food like macaroni'. The derived Latin equivalent was *pulpa*, 'flesh', which gave us the word 'pulp'.

# Purse

In Old English a *pursa* was a little leather bag in which people kept their precious coins. This was adopted from the Medieval Latin *bursa*, itself a borrowing from the Greek *bursa* (βύρσα), which did not refer to a container but to the material (stripped-off skin, hide) from which such bags were made. The associated verb *burseuein* (βυρσεύειν) meant 'to dress leather'.

Interestingly, the variants of this word became somewhat confused in English. Since the thirteenth century, for instance, the person in charge of the finances in a large institution such as a university has been referred to as a 'bursar', but on board ship the officer who performs a similar function has been known since the fifteenth century as a 'purser'.

## Pygmy

The Greek adjective *pugmaios* (πυγμαῖος), meaning 'dwarfish', was applied by the early writers Homer and Herodotos to tribes of diminutive stature who were thought to inhabit parts of Egypt, Ethiopia and India. Modern Europeans first applied the term to native peoples of equatorial Africa in the 1860s.

The origin of the word is the Greek *puks* (πύξ), 'fist', which had a derivative noun *pugmē* (πυγμή), a unit of measurement equal to approximately 1 foot 1 inch and based on the distance from a man's elbow to his knuckles. The Greeks also calculated that the distance equated to eighteen finger-widths.

## Rhapsody

Most people probably think of a rhapsody as a loosely structured and expressive piece of music, but it has only had this meaning since the mid-nineteenth century. Prior to that it was the term for an epic poem (1540s) and, since the seventeenth century, was used to describe excessively effusive expressions of emotion. The original Greek word *rhapsōdia* (ῥαψῳδία) referred either to the process of composing epic poetry or to a recital of the same. And *rhapsōdia* was a combination of the verb *rhaptein* (ῥάπτειν), 'to sew', and the noun *ōdē* (ᾠδή), 'song', so the original meaning of 'rhapsody' was something along the lines of 'songs sewn together'.


## Rhododendron

The magnificent plant known as the 'rhododendron' was first introduced from the European Alps into Britain in 1656. Its origins, however, lie in Asia where it has long been known for its beauty and thought of as a culinary delicacy. It is also the national flower of Nepal.

The word was known as early as *c.*1600 in English, from the French *rhododendron*, a direct borrowing of the Latin word of the same spelling. This had been adopted from the Greek *rhododendron* (ῥοδόδενδρον), comprising *rhodon* (ῥόδον), 'rose', and *dendron* (δένδρον), 'tree'. The literal meaning of a 'rhododenron', therefore, is a 'rose tree'.

In the Victorian language of flowers, the rhododendron stands for danger and is a warning to beware impending problems.

# Rhythm

The Latin word *rhythmus*, meaning 'timing', 'harmony', in either music or speech, made its way into English in the sixteenth century to denote almost any steady, constant movement in time. And both Latin and English adopted the Greek *rhuthmos* (ῥυθμός), which was used to define regularity and symmetry in both time and space. When applied to a person it defined his or her temper and disposition.

The verb from which the Greek noun was derived was *rhein* (ῥεῖν), 'to flow', 'to run', 'to stream'.

> *ta panta rheei kai ouden menei*
>
> τὰ πάντα ῥεει καὶ οὐδὲν μένει
>
> 'all things flow and nothing stands still'
>
> HERACLITUS OF EPHESUS

# Sandal

Normally the term denotes a light, open-toed shoe worn on the beach or anywhere when the weather is hot. The word entered English in the late fourteenth century, borrowed from the Latin *sandalium* with more or less the same meaning that we attach to it today. The Latin term was derived from the Greek *sandalon* (σάνδαλον), described as a wooden sole bound by lengths of thong to the instep and ankle of the wearer. And this word is almost certainly derived from another Greek word, *sanis* (σανίς), meaning a board, plank or just about anything made of wood.

# Sarcasm

A sarcastic remark can be either mildly offensive (and possibly amusing) or extremely hurtful and humiliating. The origin of the word, however, is even more unpleasant: it is derived from the Greek *sarks* (σάρξ), 'flesh', and the verb *sarkazein* (σαρκάζειν), 'to tear the flesh off in the manner of a dog'. Over time, the verb acquired the more figurative meaning of 'to speak to someone aggressively or bitingly'. The meaning associated with it in modern English dates from the early seventeenth century.

## Sardonic

'Sardonic' humour usually implies that the jocular remarks betray a tinge of malice or, at least, bitter sarcasm. And a person laughing 'sardonically' is usually experiencing feelings of triumphalism over and scorn for the object of his or her remarks.

The word is first recorded in English in the seventeenth century. It was adopted from the French *sardonique*, which had its origins in the Latin adjective *sardonius*; both languages had acquired the word from the Greek, although there seems to be some confusion over the spelling and etymology.

Homer used the expression *sardanion gelaein* (σαρδάνιον γελαειν), 'to laugh bitterly or scornfully', and this is possibly connected with the verb *sairein* (σαίρειν), 'to grin like a dog'. On the other hand, many etymologists are of the opinion that the connection lies with the plant *sardonion* (σαρδόνιον), which takes its name from the island where it grows in abundance, *Sardō* (Σαρδώ), Sardinia. This is an extremely bitter and poisonous plant; those who eat it contort their faces into deformed expressions such as those that accompany grim or sadistic laughter.

# Scandal

The original *skandalon* (σκάνδαλον), 'scandal', was a military implement; a snare set in order to catch one's enemies. Over time it acquired the meaning of a more figurative trap set for anyone whom we disliked or wanted to see humiliated by some momentous fall from grace. The associated verb (*skandalizein*) (σκανδαλίζειν) meant 'to trip someone up', much the same way that a politician, celebrity or indeed an ordinary member of the public can experience a humiliating 'fall' if caught up in a 'scandal'.

'Scandal' was acquired from the French *scandale* in the sixteenth century when its primary role appears to have been in a religious context. It was used to describe any discredit caused to religion by the activities or utterances of a member of a particular church. By extension, it came to mean anything discreditable, causing damage to an organization's or an individual's reputation. By the fifteenth century the associated verb 'to scandalize', meaning 'to make a public scandal', had made its entry into English.

Curiously, there is another verb 'to scandalize' with a totally unrelated meaning. In a nautical context it means 'to reduce the area of a sail'. The apparent similarity of the two verbs, however, is just that: apparent. There is absolutely no connection between the two. The sailors' word for reducing the surface area of a sail dates from the nineteenth century and is from an Old Norse term *scantle*, 'to make small'. This is related to the modern English word 'scant'.

# Sceptic

A sceptic (or, in American usage, arguably more correctly, a skeptic) is now understood to be someone who is of a naturally doubtful frame of mind. This meaning has only applied to the word, however, since 1610, as when the word first entered English in the 1580s it was used specifically to denote a member of the ancient school of Greek philosophers who taught that it was impossible to know anything with absolute certainty. It found its way into English from the Middle French *sceptique*, a borrowing from the Latin *scepticus*. And the origin of the Latin word was the Greek *skeptikos* (σκεπτικός), which simply meant 'thoughtful' or 'reflective'. The derivative verb was *skeptesthai* (σκέπτεσθαι), 'to consider', 'to think carefully about', which is 'allied to the verb *skopein* (σκοπεῖν), 'to view', 'to examine'.

# Sceptre

When William Shakespeare, in his play *King Richard II*, referred to Britain as 'this sceptred isle', he was using the word 'sceptre' as symbol of kingly authority. And, perhaps unconsciously, he was illustrating how what had originally been nothing more than a simple stick had acquired a significance far above its humble origins.

In the thirteenth century the word in English was *ceptre*, borrowed from the twelfth-century French *sceptre* and the Latin *sceptrum*, which for the Romans was a term

## PYRRHŌ

Pyrrho of Elis was a philosopher of the Hellenistic period who had been a soldier in Alexander the Great's army and followed him halfway across the known world and took part in the conquest of India. No doubt when he was not fighting, Pyrrhō was doing a lot of thinking since, on his return to Greece, he is believed to have founded the philosophers' group known as *hoi skeptikoi* (οἱ σκεπτικοί), 'the Sceptics'. They consistently refused to assert anything positively and would never do any more than express an opinion, as they believed that this was the limit of an individual's intellectual scope.

They also borrowed from the Epicureans the conviction that the correct course one should adopt through life was one of *ataraxia*, 'calmness achieved through mastery of, or freedom from, one's passions'.

for a staff of office but could also be used as a metaphor for 'dominion', 'kingdom' or 'royal authority'. This usage had been acquired from the Greeks, who used the term for the baton of authority carried by rulers and heralds. Speakers in ancient Athens, also, when they stood up to address a gathering of citizens, would be handed a baton as a sign that they had the floor and should be allowed to speak and be heard.

But the symbol of authority was known in Greek as a *skēptron* (σκῆπτρον), and, despite its later elevated significance, was originally nothing more than a piece of old stick used to support its owner. Its derivative verb was *skēptein* (σκήπτειν), meaning simply 'to shore up', 'to support'.

It has also been suggested that the Greek noun and verb could be distantly related to the English 'shaft'.

## Schedule

The word 'schedule' has only been used as a synonym for 'timetable' since the railways adopted it for the benefit of their passengers in 1863. The origin of the word can be traced back to the Latin *schedula* and the Romans' use of it to denote a strip of papyrus. The Romans borrowed the term from the Greek *schedē* (σχέδη), also a strip of papyrus but originally nothing more than a 'splinter' or 'cleft piece of wood'. The derivative verb here was *schizein* (σχίζειν), 'to split', suggesting that the first 'schedules' could have been strips of wood or papyrus used by the Greeks to make notes or remind themselves of what they had to do or where they had to be on a given date.

## School

Despite the feverish activity, particularly as examinations loom, associated with the modern concept of a school, the original derivative Greek word *scholē* (σχολή) meant 'leisure'! In fifth-century Athens only the sons of the idle rich had time on their hands when they could indulge their favourite pastimes, and for many this meant sitting in the sunshine listening to the learned men of the day (the 'philosophers', or 'lovers of wisdom') as they waxed lyrical about the meaning of life and so on.

Eventually such leisure activity came to be associated with not only listening to the great thinkers but studying and analysing what they had to say. And this led to almost every European language adopting the Greek word for leisure, in one form or another, to designate a place of instruction and learning.

## Seismic

Politicians and political commentators like to use the word 'seismic' when some event has major implications for society and perhaps alters the historical direction in which the country has been travelling. For the sake of literary or rhetorical variety they might alter their vivid descriptions to include the phrases 'earth-shattering' or 'groundbreaking', perhaps unaware that, etymologically, all these descriptive conceits are very close to the original Greek idea.

In the nineteenth century an engineer, John Milne, who was working on earthquake early-warning systems, invented a machine that could detect the tremors in the Earth which acted as a strong indicator that an earthquake was imminent or at least likely to happen

## POSEIDŌN

According to the Ancient Greeks, the god responsible for earthquakes was Poseidōn, known to the Romans as Neptune.

Of course, most people think of Poseidōn as the god of the sea and oceans. As the son of Cronos and Rhea and brother of Zeus and Hades, he lived in the depths of the sea off the coast of Euboea where he kept horses with brazen hooves and golden manes. When he took these horses out for a canter over the waves they had a strangely calming effect on the surface of the waters, and so it was to Poseidōn that the hapless seafarer prayed when terrified by a violent storm. His affinity with horses, in fact, was thought to be so close that he is credited in Greek mythology with creating the first horse that ever lived.

Most people are familiar with Poseidōn's famous symbol of power, the trident. But how many know what uses he put it to? The trident was not just a symbol; the god used it to break up rocks, cause or subdue storms, or – as and when the whim took him – shake the Earth, creating the earthquakes which brought misery to mortals.

fairly soon. Obviously, he had to think of a name for his invention, and in 1880 resorted to Greek, which had the noun *seismos* (σεισμός), which meant 'shaking', 'shock' or 'earthquake', and was itself derived from the verb *seiein* (σείειν), 'to shake'.

He then added the suffix 'graph' from the Greek verb *graphein* (γράφειν), 'to write', and the resultant noun was 'seismograph', literally a machine which produced written evidence of an impending or occurring earthquake.

## Septic

At some time around 1600 the word 'septic' crept into English as an adjective used to describe wounds and flesh that had become infected and were in the process of decay. Its roots can be traced back to the Ancient Greeks, who used the words *sēpsis* (σῆψις) and *sēpedōn* (σηπεδών) when referring to rotten or rotting flesh. The associated verb *sēpesthai* (σήπεσθαι) meant 'to rot'.

By 1750 the word 'anti-septic' had been coined to describe any concoction or supposed cure for an insect bite or festering wound, and by 1803 the word was being used as a noun so that it became possible to talk of 'an anti-septic', just as we do today. The word 'anti-septic' simply comprises the basic Greek adjective with the addition of the prefix *anti-* (ἀντι-), 'against'.

# Siren

In the modern world a siren is associated with strident, high-pitched alarms emanating from police cars, ambulances or the devices on buildings warning the populace of an impending emergency. The common denominator here is the strident noise intended to induce the flow of adrenalin and make people run for their lives or take shelter.

The original sirens, however, were spirits of the sea with the bodies of birds and the faces of beautiful women who enchanted sailors with their seductive singing and enticed them to sail closer and closer to the source of the divine music until they crashed onto the rocks and were slain.

The Greek name for these treacherously alluring females was *Seirenes* (Σειρῆνες). Homer tells us that when Odysseus sailed near to their island he made his crew stuff wax into their ears so they would not hear the delightful, enticing sounds. He, on the other hand, lashed himself to the mast as this would allow him to hear the sweet music but prevent him from succumbing to its charms.

'Sirens' first entered English in the fourteenth century as mythical female monsters with seductive voices. By the sixteenth century the term was being applied to people thought of as dangerously attractive. As an alarm or device warning of impending danger the word dates from 1879.

It has been argued that the singular form of the word, *seiren*, is connected with *seira*, 'rope', 'cord', 'lasso', and that the Sirens' singing resembled a metaphorical lasso with which to ensnare their victims. If this is the etymology of the word, there is a wonderful irony in the account of Odysseus lashing himself to the mast: the Sirens attempted to ensnare Odysseus with a metaphorical rope but he used an actual one to resist them.

## Skeleton

The Greeks passed this word on to us, even though they attached a different meaning to it. *Skeleton* (σκελετόν) was a noun derived from the adjective *skeletos* (σκελετός), 'parched', 'dried up', which was frequently combined with the word for a 'body', *sōma* (σῶμα), to produce their term for what we would now refer to as a 'mummy'. The Greeks never used the word to designate the bony framework of a human or animal's body; this usage followed the word's absorption into English in the 1570s.

## Sketch

In the seventeenth century the Italian word *schizzo* (a brief sketch, from the verb *schizzare*, 'to dash off a quick drawing') made its way into English with the spelling we associate with it still today. The Italian version was a later form of the Latin *schedius*, also an 'off-the-cuff drawing', borrowed from the Greek word *schedios* (σχέδιος), a noun meaning 'something dashed off with whatever is at hand'. And this is where we come face to face with the origin of the word: the Greek adverb *schedon* (σχεδόν), 'near-by', 'close-at-hand', and the derivative verb *schediazō* (σχεδιάζω), 'to make something with whatever is lying at hand'.

Presumably, with all the advantages of modern technology, our modern-day parliamentary 'sketch writers' are a little better prepared and no longer have to rely on writing implements 'lying within reach' before they can entertain us with their witty asides and pertinent observations.

## *Sophisticated*

'Sophisticated' has only been used as a synonym for 'urbane', 'cultured' or 'refined' since relatively recent times. In the eighteenth century it meant 'deprived of simplicity', but further back, around 1600, a 'sophisticated' person was thought of as corrupt and liable to deceive by misleading or spurious argument.

The word's chequered history began in ancient Athens where the word *sophos* (σοφός) meant 'wise' and a *sophistēs* (σοφιστής) was 'a wise man' or 'a teacher'. Over time, however, as these teachers realized they could earn a decent living out of their craft, they began charging for their services. This move, combined with their claimed ability to make men wise and to argue the cause of whoever was paying the most, brought them into disrepute. In particular they incurred the displeasure of Socrates and Plato.

An associated word in English is 'sophistry', the ability to reason with clever but totally fallacious arguments designed to deceive or misguide.


## Spasm

As a medical term, 'spasm' was absorbed into English in the fourteenth century, borrowed from the French *spasme*, a 'cramp'. This can be traced back ultimately to the Greek *spasma* (σπάσμα), which, depending on the context, could be anything from a sprain to a rupture of muscular fibre, or even a convulsion. The verb concerned here is *span* (σπᾶν), meaning 'to draw', 'to pluck' or, more specifically and appropriately here, 'to pull tight'.

In the seventeenth century the adjective 'spasmodic' made its appearance in English with reference to medical afflictions marked by 'spasms' or uncontrollable twitching. And the unpredictability of such episodes led to a further development in the use of the adjective as an alternative to 'intermittent' in the nineteenth century.

## Sporadic

Now applied to almost anything occurring at irregular intervals, this is another word that has its origins in the world of Greek agriculture and farming. The Greek adjective was *sporadikos* (σποραδικός), meaning 'scattered' or 'sown', derived from the verb *speirein* (σπείρειν), 'to sow'. The same verb has also given us (i) the word 'spore', which since the nineteenth century has defined the minute reproductive bodies in plants that have no flowers, and (ii) the name of the group of 'scattered' islands in the Aegean Sea known as the Sporades (Σποράδες).

The word was first recorded in English in the seventeenth century.

## Squirrel

'Squirrel' entered English in the early fourteenth century, having crossed the English Channel from France, which had the word *escuruel*, a borrowing from the Latin *scurius*. But the Latin word was itself an adaptation of the Greek *skiouros* (σκίουρος), a contraction of *skia* (σκιά), 'shadow', and *oura* (οὐρά), 'tail'. A 'squirrel', then, is simply an animal whose tail casts a shadow.

## Stigma

When 'stigma' entered the English language in around the year 1400 it was spelled *stigme*; the form that we recognize today was a later development and did not appear until the 1590s. At that time it was not used in a figurative sense at all, its meaning being restricted to a 'mark made with a red-hot poker'.

It entered English from the Latin *stigma*, which in turn had been borrowed from the Greek *stigma* (στίγμα), a noun derived from the verb *stizein* (στίζειν), 'to brand', 'to mark'. These were words used in animal husbandry where normal practice was to mark cattle with the owner's distinctive mark or brand. But, on a more gruesome level, such words would have featured also in the vocabulary of those involved in the slave trade. Runaway slaves in Ancient Greece, if they were caught, were marked or branded, no doubt as a deterrent to other captives who might have been entertaining the idea of escape.

The metaphorical use of the word 'stigma' as a sign of disgrace for some lapse of behaviour or moral standard dates only from *c.*1610. The 'stigmata' of Christ's wounds appearing mysteriously and inexplicably on the hands of the religiously devout was first mentioned in the 1630s.

## Stoical

In the late fourteenth century, when English acquired the term 'stoical' from the Latin *stoicus*, its use was confined to descriptions of anything or anyone associated with the Ancient Greek school of philosophy founded by Zeno. By the 1570s the word was being more widely used and applied to just about anybody who could withstand pain or discomfort without complaining or revealing to others what they were enduring. Modern synonymous expressions typifying a stoical attitude include 'stiff upper lip', 'taking it on the chin' and 'manning up'.

The Latin *stoicus* was taken from the Greek *stōikos* (στωικός). This, like its fourteenth-century English equivalent, was descriptive of Zeno's followers, but its original meaning was more architectural than philosophical. The Greek word *stoa* (στοά) was basically a 'column' (literally 'something standing') but was applied more generally to any colonnaded square or cloister.

ZENO

Zeno of Citium was born on Cyprus *c*.335 BCE and died in Athens, some time around the year 263 BCE. He was intensely interested in ethics, physics and logic, and is generally considered one of the leading Greek philosophers. He believed that the path to true happiness was one of simplicity, if not austerity, combined with a harmonious relationship with what Fate has to offer. He taught that virtue and knowledge were connected and that only a wise man could be considered virtuous. One of the main tenets of his teaching was that *kathēkon* (καθῆκον), 'the correct action to suit the circumstance', was all-important.

Zeno conducted his classes in the *Stoa Poikilē*, or Painted Colonnade, and his students were known originally as *hoi ek tēs stoas* (οι ἔκ τῆς στοᾶς), 'the boys from the colonnade'. This was soon shortened to 'the Stoics'.

# Stomach

The area of the body defined by this word has shifted its position slightly over the years. Since the fourteenth century it has defined the sack or pouch beneath the heart where all food is digested and processed before being excreted. In Middle English it was known as the *stomak*, an adaptation of the Old French *stomaque*, both of which were taken from the Latin *stomachus*. But *stomachus*, like the Greek noun from which it was derived, *stomachos* (στόμαχος), meant 'throat' or 'gullet'. And the Greek noun was derived from another word, *stoma* (στόμα), 'mouth'.

The part of the body we now understand as the 'stomach' was referred to by the Ancient Greeks as the *gastēr* (γαστήρ), which explains words used in modern medical terminology such as 'gastric', 'gastritis' and, the name by which a man or woman who likes their food is known, 'gastronome'.

# Strategy

Now used frequently as a synonym for an 'overall plan' the word 'strategy' was restricted to military contexts when it entered English in the early part of the nineteenth century. English borrowed it from the French, who had acquired the Greek term *strategia* (στρατηγία), applied to the responsibilities and duties of a military officer equating, in modern terms, to a *stratēgos* (στρατηγός), or general. As a general's main task has always been to plan

## THE GENERALS

The Athenians, in the fifth century BCE, had what we would now consider a very odd system for appointing senior military commanders (*stratēgoi*). A modern general will almost certainly have spent many years in the forces acquiring skills and knowledge appropriate to various junior and senior officer posts as he worked his way up through the chain of command. In Athens, however, the ten top military vacancies were filled by election. Consequently, a citizen doing his duty could find himself serving as an ordinary foot soldier in one war (or battle) and then as a general in the next, and vice versa. Presumably this was a case of the Greek concept of democracy being taken perhaps more than just a little too far.

for the overall conduct of a war, 'strategy' has come to signify leadership and an ability to plan ahead in both military and civilian contexts.

The Greek word for a 'general' comprises two elements: *stratos* (στρατός), 'army', and *agein* (ἄγειν), 'to lead', so the literal meaning of the word is 'leader of an army'.

## Surgeon

A 'doctor' or 'general practitioner' tends to be someone who examines us when we are ill and advises us on what to do or what pills to take. A 'surgeon', on the other hand, is more likely to cut us open in order to perform delicate operations demanding skill and dexterity.

For a clue to the origin of the word we have to go all the way back to Latin, which had *chirurgia*, 'surgery', which in turn came from the Greek *cheirourgia* (χειρουργία), a combination of *cheir* (χείρ), 'hand', and *ergon* (ἔργον), 'work'. Literally, then, 'surgery' is just 'handiwork' or its Latin-based English equivalent, 'manual labour'. The word entered English in the fourteenth century.


# Sycophant

There are two parts to the discussion about the origin of this word. Etymologists agree that the original Greek *sukophantes* (συκοφάντης) comprised two elements: *sukon* (σῦκον), 'fig', and *phainein* (φαίνειν), 'to show', and so literally meant 'fig-shower'. Why a 'fig-shower' should be associated with bootlicking toadyism is however unclear, and etymologists are yet to agree on a definitive explanation.

In ancient Athens the *sukophantai* were semi-professional informers who made a living out of reporting on miscreants, who then found themselves answering charges in court. At least some of the time these informers were attempting to curry favour with the authorities by denouncing people involved in the illegal trade of exporting figs, a commodity so highly prized in Athens that its sale abroad was strictly forbidden. But the prohibition bred smugglers, and smuggling bred people willing to 'grass', thereby ingratiating themselves with the authorities. It is just possible (but the theory is disputed) that the 'fig-showers' were originally the informers who would show the authorities where the figs were stored prior to being transported out of Athens. Such 'sycophancy' was intended to win favour and no doubt bring personal gain.

## Syllabus

There seems to be a good deal of confusion among etymologists when it comes to the derivation of the word 'syllabus'. Most seem to agree that it was used in English as early as the 1650s to refer to a table of contents for series of lectures and so on. They all seem to agree also that this meaning came from the Late Latin use of the word simply meaning 'list' and that this was ultimately a misreading of the Greek *sittubos* (σίττυβος), 'a parchment label' or 'table of contents'.

But the most authoritative Greek dictionary (Liddell & Scott) informs us that *sittubos* (σίττυβος) was the Greek for a 'three-legged stool', which hardly seems relevant here. The same source tells us also that there was a Greek word *sillubos* (σίλλυβος), which was either a kind of edible thistle (obviously not applicable here either) or 'a parchment label, appended to the outside of a book' and the equivalent of the Latin *index*. It would seem more than reasonable to assume that this is the derivation of our 'syllabus' and that no misreading was ever involved.

This assumption is further supported by another authority (Wyld), who states that the noun is derived from the verb *sullambanein* (συλλαμβάνειν), 'to gather together'. This makes sense if we consider that a college 'syllabus', for example, gathers together all the courses available to students and presents them in a concise list.

## Symposium

This word has made two entries into English. In the sixteenth century it was adopted as the Latinized form of the Greek *Sumposion* or *Symposion* (Συμπόσιον), the title of one of Plato's *Dialogues*. It was a combination of *sun* or *syn* (σύν), 'with', 'together', and *posis* (πόσις), 'drinking', from the verb *pinein* (πίνειν), 'to drink', for as far back as the fifth century BCE the Greeks had discovered the pleasure of combining intellectual discussion with the convivial partaking of a cup or three of wine!

The modern usage defining a gathering of like-minded people intent on serious conversation and discussion dates from the eighteenth century.

## Symptom

The modern meaning of 'symptom' as evidence that something has occurred or that a change has taken place is a relatively new development. It has only been applicable in a non-medical context since the early seventeenth century. In the 1540s, when it found its way into English, it meant 'accident', 'disease' or 'happening'.

Its Greek derivative noun was *sumptōma* (σύμπτωμα), which was made up of the prefix *sum-* or *sym-* (συμ-), 'with', and the verb *piptein* (πίπτειν), 'to fall'. The composite verb *sumpiptein* (συμπίπτειν) is normally translated as 'to happen', but we get a better idea of the literal meaning if we equate it with the now rather archaic verb 'to befall'. The original 'symptom' therefore was an occurrence that had 'befallen' someone rather than an indication of a possible problem requiring medical attention.

When a patient presents with symptoms pointing to a particular disease it is normal to speak of a 'syndrome', as in 'Asperger's syndrome' or 'Down's syndrome'. The same Greek prefix is in play here, but now linked with *dromos* (δρόμος), 'running', from the verb *dramein* (δραμεῖν), 'to run'. Thus a 'syndrome' defines several indicators all 'running together' to reveal a particular medical condition.

# Syringe

These days we probably think of a syringe as a modified tube designed specifically for injecting fluid of one sort or another into the arm of a doctor's patient. To the Ancient Greeks, however, a *surigks* (σῦριγξ), 'syringe', was just about anything resembling a pipe, including a shepherd's pipe, a spear case and the anatomical windpipe. What we now refer to as 'pan pipes' were also referred to as 'syringes'.

The word was adopted into English in the fifteenth century from the Late Latin *syringe*, which had borrowed it from the Greek. It was first applied to hypodermic (Greek for 'under the skin') needles in 1884.

### SYRINX

In Greek mythology Syrinx was an Arcadian nymph who caught the eye of Pan, the pastoral god, but – being less than enthusiastic about the fate that awaited her – she fled from his amorous advances. When it became obvious that he was not easily discouraged, she jumped into the River Ladon and metamorphosed into a reed protruding from the surface of the water. No doubt feeling somewhat disappointed and frustrated, Pan cut off the reed, fashioned it into a flute of sorts, then derived comfort and solace in the soothing music it produced.

## Tantalize

If we find something tantalizing we are saying that it attracts us; we want it but it is teasingly unobtainable. For an explanation of the term we have to go back to Greek mythology, which informs us that *Tantalos* (Τάνταλος), the king of Phrygia, was punished for incurring the displeasure of the gods. His punishment involved being sent down to the underworld, where he was condemned to stand in water that receded as soon as he tried to drink from it. Perhaps even more 'tantalizing' was the fruit hanging above his head, which moved just out of reach when he extended a hand to seize it.

Directly related to this tale is the Victorian invention known as a 'tantalus'. This is a specially designed holder for two or three decanters (usually a combination of whisky, port and sherry) clearly visible but securely locked away. The original idea was that, in well-to-do households, such a contraption would prevent the servants from getting their hands on the precious liquid within. Only the keyholder could undo the lock and gain access to the decanters; everyone else remained 'tanatalized' by the sight of the unattainable liquor.

## Technical

In modern English, the adjective 'technical' applies in most contexts to machinery or mechanics. When the word found its way into English in the early seventeenth

## PANTECHNICON

Most people today hearing the word 'pantechnicon' will think of the huge delivery wagons that thunder along our roads, delivering vast amounts of consumer goods to shops and supermarkets. But the original 'pantechnicon' was a building, not a vehicle.

In the nineteenth century a couple of enterprising brothers opened an unbelievably well-stocked establishment in London, which must have seemed like an Aladdin's cave to its customers. This soon became the place to go if you wanted to buy furniture or a new horse-drawn carriage, or simply find a suitably large picture to adorn a dining-room wall. As such a wide variety of objects were on sale, the owners decided that Pantechnicon (in Greek, 'all the arts and skills') would be a suitably descriptive name for their premises. As business boomed, of course, the brothers realized that they now needed very large vehicles to collect and deliver the goods and artefacts from and to various parts of London. Included in the design of such wagons was the name 'Pantechnicon van' written in large letters down each side.

Unfortunately, the building was destroyed by fire in 1874, but the vans survived and could still be seen weaving their way in and out of the traffic on the thoroughfares of the capital. For a while the term 'pantechnicon van' continued to be used among the general populace, but eventually all large vehicles used for the distribution of goods far and wide acquired the name we know them by today, pantechnicons.

century, however, it would have been applied to anyone displaying a particular aptitude or skill. The narrower meaning, suggesting a connection with mechanical devices or defining someone who is 'good with their hands', dates from the 1720s.

The Greek adjective, from which the word derives, is *technikos* (τεχνικός), 'skilful', from *technē* (τέχνη), a noun with a multitude of meanings. It could mean all of: skill, craft, cunning device, trick or wile, and trade. It even included what we would now think of as 'art', which explains the Greek saying (attributed to Hippocrates):

*ho bios brachus, hē technē makra*

ὁ βίος βραχύς, ἡ τέχνη μακρά

'life is short, art is long'

## Telephone

The Scottish engineer Alexander Graham Bell is credited with inventing or developing a device in the nineteenth century which would allow people to talk to each other over long distances. When he was searching for a name for this wonderful new contraption he turned to Greek. As his invention involved people communicating remotely by voice, he combined the two Greek words, *tēle* (τῆλε), an adverb meaning 'far off', 'at a distance', and *phōnē* (φωνή), 'sound', 'voice'. Putting them together, he added a new word to the English dictionary, 'telephone'.

Other 'tele-' words:

| | |
|---:|:---|
| *telegraph or telegram* | written at a distance |
| *telepathy* | sensed at a distance |
| *telekinesis* | moved at a distance |
| *television* | seen at a distance |
| | (*vision* is Latin) |
| *telescope* | seen at a distance |

And *phōnē*, of course, is the word that also gave us 'phonetics', the science of speech and sound, in the nineteenth century.


# Theatre

People have enjoyed going to the theatre throughout the world for thousands of years. One of the favourite pastimes for people in Ancient Greece was to gather in the open air, no doubt in the cool of the evening, to watch a play by Euripides or Sophocles or a number of minor playwrights whose names history has failed to record.

The Greek term for the place where the populace gathered to see the latest play was *theatron* (θέατρον), which, with a very slight change of spelling, has given us our word 'theatre'. The Greek noun was derived from the verb *theasthai* (θεᾶσθαι), 'to view', 'to gaze at', and so the *theatron* was literally the place where people went 'to view' or 'gaze at' whatever was taking place on the stage.

Until the fourteenth century, theatrical productions in Britain were often staged on areas of open ground or on market squares for the entertainment and edification of the local populace. And well into the fifteenth century, inn courtyards often served as a venue where travelling actors could put on their latest productions. The idea of a fixed, dedicated building known as a 'theatre' did not occur until the sixteenth century.

The phrase 'theatre of war' is not recorded before 1914.


## Therapy

In Ancient Greece the verb *therapeuein* (θεραπεύειν) had several meanings. It could mean (i) to wait on, to attend, to serve, (ii) to pay service to the gods, and (iii) to till the land.

But it also had another meaning, the one that has made its way into English: to tend the sick, to heal, to cure. The noun associated with this verb was *therapeia* (θεραπεία), meaning 'attendance', 'serving' or 'tending the sick'. Another derivative noun, *therapōn* (θεράπων), was the term for an attendant or servant, although in Homer (*c.*700 BCE) it meant 'a companion in arms'.

'Therapy' as an alternative term to 'medical treatment' entered English in the nineteenth century.

> *iatre, therapeuson seauton*
>
> ἰατρέ, θεράπευσον σεαυτόν
>
> 'physician, heal thyself'

LUKE 4:23

## Thrombosis

People who fly long distances are now advised to wear elasticated (and very uncomfortable) stockings in order to avoid the potentially life-threatening condition known as 'deep vein thrombosis'.

The more general term 'thrombosis' has been used in English since long before mankind learned to fly; in fact it was first recorded in 1706 when it was borrowed from the Modern Latin *thrombosis*. No doubt the medieval doctors had recognized that lumps or swellings in various parts of the body could lead to all sorts of medical problems and even a heart attack and death. But it was the Greeks who gave the medical fraternity the word, as their *thrombos* (θρόμβος) meant 'a lump', particularly of the type observed in milk when it turns sour. Another related noun, *thrombōsis* (θρόμβωσις), meant 'curdling', and *thrombōsis galaktos* (θρόμβωσις γάλακτος) was specifically 'curdled milk'.

## Thyme

What could be more quintessentially English than an abundance of rosemary and thyme flourishing in a country garden? But why is 'thyme' pronounced to rhyme with 'time?'

In the fourteenth century we borrowed the word from the French, who pronounced it as 'teem' (they can't reproduce the English 'th' sound); they in turn had acquired

it centuries earlier from the Greeks, whose term for the sweet-smelling herb they burned when offering sacrifice to the gods was *thumos or thumon* (θύμος or θυμόν). And the herb took its name from the verb *thuein* (θυειν), 'to worship', 'to sacrifice'.

Believe it or not, the Greeks also used a similar sounding, but possibly unrelated, *thumos* (θυμός) as one of their words for the soul, the life force and passion.

## Toxic

'Toxic' is now virtually synonymous with 'poisonous', but it has come down to us from the Greek word for a bow (as in archery). It made its way into English from the Latin *toxicum*, 'poison', itself a borrowing from the Greek *toxikon pharmakon* (τοξικόν φάρμακον), 'poisonous compound for use by archers'. There has been a slight shift in meaning here as, although the word *toxon* referred to the bow, the 'poisonous compound' was used for covering the arrowheads before firing them at an enemy.

The same root also produced the verb 'to intoxicate'. A person suffering from (or enjoying) the effects of alcohol has been described in English as 'intoxicated' since the sixteenth century.

## Tragedy

It may come as something of a surprise but this word has come down to us from the Greek *tragos* (τράγος), meaning a 'male goat'. In Ancient Greece competitions were frequently held to see who could write the best play. There are two theories as to how the goat acquired its association with serious drama as opposed to comedy. The first is that it was the custom for actors in plays dealing with serious themes to wear goatskins; the second is that the playwright responsible for the best production was awarded a goat as a prize.

The word entered English in the fourteenth century, applied to dramatic pieces on stage with a disastrous ending; by the sixteenth century it was being used generally outside the theatre to describe any calamitous event.

## Treacle

The sweet, sticky black substance we associate with this word has come a long way from its original meaning. We now use it mainly in bakery, but in the Middle Ages it was thought of as an antidote for poison and was administered to people who had been bitten by a snake or wild animal.

The first thing to say about the word's derivation, however, is: forget the 'l'. It should not be there; it is what linguists refer to as an 'intrusive' consonant, being apparently a Provençal dialect addition. The Old French word was '*triacle*' from the Latin *theriaca* and, further back, the Greek *theriakē* (θηριαχή), an adjective derived from *thēr* (θήρ), 'wild animal'.

Such was the faith in the efficacy of the substance in Ancient Greece that anyone bitten by a snake or wild beast was immediately given a dose of *theriakē antidotos* (θεριαχή ἀντίδοτος), an antidote against the bite of a poisonous animal. Just how successful such administrations were we cannot be sure.


## Trophy

The Greeks took their fighting very seriously. Not only did they consider it shameful to turn and run away from the battlefield once defeat became a distinct possibility, but they also considered it vital to take home proof of their victories.

The verb *trepein* (τρέπειν) in Greek meant 'to turn'; if an adversary 'turned' and fled, dropping his shield and sword, these became battlefield detritus, collectively known as *tropaia* (τροπαῖα), to be picked up by the victorious forces and hung on trees or posts as evidence of their conquest. Hence the *tropaion* (τρόπαιον) (singular of *tropaia*), or 'trophy', became a symbol of victory gained when the enemy 'turned' and ran away. Nowadays, of course, 'trophies' are awarded for prowess in sporting contests rather than on the field of mortal combat.

The word 'trophy' has existed in English as a symbol of victory since the sixteenth century.

## Truck

The use of this word in English to designate a wheeled vehicle to carry goods dates only from the eighteenth century. Prior to that it meant a small, solid wooden wheel, particularly of the type found in pulleys. In fact, the common pulley is where we have to look for the derivation of the word. In Greek, a pulley wheel was referred to as a *trochilea* (τροχῖλέα), derived from *trochos* (τροχος), 'wheel', and the verb *trechein* (τρέχειν), 'to run'. Perhaps the basic idea is that, even for the Ancient Greeks, wheels were thought of as making vehicles 'run' more smoothly.

The expression 'to have (no) truck with' has nothing whatever to do with wheels or pulleys. It is simply from an Old French word *troquer*, 'to barter' or 'do business with'.

# Typhoon

There is a certain amount of discussion concerning the derivation of this word. Folk etymologists suggest that its origins lie in the region of the South China seas and that the word is a corruption of the Chinese *tai fung*, 'great wind', the expression supposedly being adopted by European sailors who traded in that part of the world in the sixteenth century. It has also been suggested that the word made its way into English, also in the sixteenth century, from the Arabic *tūfān*, 'hurricane' or 'tornado'.

The similarity with the Chinese expression is almost certainly coincidental (the words sound alike but there is no etymological link), but the Arabic is possibly a borrowing from the Greek *tuphōn* (τυφῶν), 'great storm', 'furious wind', a noun derived from the verb *tuphein* (τύφειν), 'to raise smoke or mist'. The comparison here is no doubt with the 'smoky' appearance of the vast dust clouds that accompany violent storms in that part of the world.

Interestingly, the verb *tuphein* also gave us the medical term 'typhus', a disease characterized by the patient's high fever and 'misty' or 'smoky' vision.

## A WINDY GIANT

In Greek mythology, of course, virtually all natural events were personified as superhuman beings, and so *tŭphōn* became *Tŭphōs*, a monstrous giant who generated violent storms and wanted to destroy the world. When Zeus attempted to thwart his nefarious intentions, Tŭphōs threw him down into a ravine, whence he had to be rescued by Pan and Hermēs before he could recover from his injuries and defeat the dreadful monster.

# Tyrant

Since it found its way into English in the thirteenth century, the word 'tyrant' has always had negative connotations and designated any ruler who used cruel, oppressive or despotic methods in order to keep the people down and to retain power.

The original Greek word, *turannos* (τύραννος), however, had a more precise meaning: it was applied to any ruler who had assumed power by the forceful overthrow of a legitimate monarch. Some of these usurpers were fairly despotic and unscrupulous, but it was also perfectly possible to be a 'tyrant' and rule in a generous and democratic manner.

## A BENEVOLENT TYRANT

One tyrant in particular stood out in ancient Athens as an intelligent man who had the interests of his people at heart. This was Peisistratos, who governed Athens at various times between 561 and 527 BCE and died in 528/7. He was officially a 'tyrant' but most of his policies and achievements are more in keeping with the kind of statesman we would associate with social democracy rather than tyranny. He championed the lower classes by, for instance, confiscating land from the aristocracy and distributing it among the populace, and he also lowered taxes. In addition to this he had the brilliant idea of creating a body of men we would refer to as 'circuit judges', who travelled around the area providing ordinary citizens with access to justice.

Peisistratos was also a staunch supporter of the arts. He instructed scholars to produce a definitive version of the works of Homer and did much to enhance the architectural beauty of Athens. Under his stewardship the theatre, sculpture and the arts in general all flourished.

## *Xylophone*

Various forms of the musical instrument known as the 'xylophone' have been around for centuries, and there is evidence that the first ones were being played in South East Asia as early as the ninth century. The European model appeared in the nineteenth century and the word itself was coined in 1866.

As a musical instrument, it is a member of the percussion family, consisting of a series of wooden bars of varying lengths, played by being struck by mallets. And the 'wooden' bars here are a clue to the derivation of the word. It is derived from two Greek words, *ksulon* (ξύλον), 'wood' or 'tree', and *phōnē* (φωνή), 'sound'.

Originally, *ksulon* was simply 'wood', once it was ready for its intended use; so firewood, timber and so on could be referred to as *ksulon*, but so too could a bench or table, especially of the type used by money changers. In the theatres of ancient Athens, the VIP seat right at the front was referred to as the *prōton ksulon* (πρῶτον ξύλον), literally 'the first bench', and would have been reserved for the great and the good of Athenian society.

## Zoo

The world's first scientific zoo was opened in London in the nineteenth century by the Zoological Society. The name was derived from the Greek *zōon* (ζῷον), 'animal', the root of other words associated with animals such as 'zoology' (the study of animals) and 'zoolatry' (the worship of animals). It also explains why all the signs of the Zodiac or *zōdiakos kuklos* (ζωδιακός κύκλος), 'zodiac circle', are animals (of both the biped and quadruped varieties).

*ho anthrōpos politikon zōon estin*

ὁ ἄνθρωπος πολιτικόν ζῷον ἐστιν

'man is a political animal'

ARISTOTLE

# FURTHER READING
## AND SOURCES

Allen, James Turney. *Super Review of Classical/Ancient Greek.* Research and Education Association, Piscataway NJ, 2001.

Autenrieth, Georg. *A Homeric Dictionary.* Translated by Robert P. Keep. Macmillan, London, 1960.

Ayto, John. *Dictionary of Word Origins.* Bloomsbury, London, 1990.

Betts, Gavin, and Alan Henry. *Ancient Greek.* Hodder & Stoughton, London, 2001.

Burn, A.R. *The Penguin History of Greece.* Penguin, Harmondsworth, 1985.

Chernykh, P.Ya. *Istoriko-etimologicheskiy slovar' russkogo yazyka* [Historical etymological dictionary of the Russian language]. Russkiy yazyk, Moscow, 2001.

Harper, Douglas. *On-line Etymological Dictionary.* 2001–. www.etymonline.com/bio.php.

Hawkins, Joyce M. (ed.). *The Oxford Reference Dictionary.* Oxford University Press, London, 1991.

Hoad, T.F. (ed.). *Concise Oxford Dictionary of English Etymology.* Oxford University Press, Oxford, 1996.

JACT. *Reading Greek.* Cambridge University Press, Cambridge, 2008.

————— *The World of Athens,* 2nd edn. Cambridge University Press, Cambridge, 2008.

Jones, Peter. *Eureka!* Atlantic Books, London, 2014.

Kitto, H.D.F. *The Greeks.* Penguin, Harmondsworth, 1962.

Liddell, Henry George, and Robert Scott. *Greek–English Lexicon.* Clarendon Press, Oxford, 1963 [1864].

Mavromataki, Maria. *Greek Mythology and Religion*. Editions Haitalis, Athens, 1997.

McArthur, Tom. *The Oxford Companion to the English Language*. Oxford University Press, Oxford, 1992.

Russell, Bertrand. *A History of Western Philosophy*. Allen & Unwin, London, 1985.

Shipley, Joseph T. *The Origins of English Words*. Johns Hopkins University Press, Baltimore MD, 1984.

Simpson, D.P. *Cassell's New Latin–English, English–Latin Dictionary*. Cassell, London, 1959.

Skeat, Walter W. *The Concise Dictionary of English Etymology*. Wordsworth Reference, Ware, 1993.

———*An Etymological Dictionary of the English Language,* Clarendon Press, Oxford, 1974.

Stobart, J.C. *The Glory That Was Greece*. Book Club Associates, London, 1972.

Thompson, Della (ed.). *The Concise Oxford Dictionary,* 9th edn. Oxford University Press, Oxford, 1995.

Thomson, George. *The Greek Language*. W. Heffer & Sons, Cambridge, 1960.

Tulloch, Alexander. *Word Routes; Journeys through Etymology*. Peter Owen, London, 2005.

——— *Understanding English Homonyms: Their Origins and Usage*. Hong Kong University Press, Hong Kong, 2017.

Wyld, Henry Cecil (ed.). *The Universal Dictionary of the English Language*. Waverley, London, 1956.